THE PENGUIN BOOK OF AMERICAN FOLK SONGS

ALAN LOMAX

Q 19

The Penguin Book of American Folk Songs

COMPILED AND EDITED WITH NOTES BY

ALAN LOMAX

PIANO ARRANGEMENTS BY ELIZABETH POSTON

PENGUIN BOOKS

Penguin Books Ltd, Harmondsworth, Middlesex, England
Penguin Books Inc., 7110 Ambassador Road, Baltimore, Maryland 21207, U.S.A.
Penguin Books Australia Ltd, Ringwood, Victoria, Australia

First published 1964
Reprinted 1966, 1968, 1971

Copyright © Alan Lomax, 1964
Piano arrangements copyright © Elizabeth Poston, 1964

Made and printed in Great Britain by
Lowe & Brydone (Printers) Ltd, London
Set in Monotype Times

CONTENTS

Contents

ACKNOWLEDGEMENTS

From *American Ballads and Folk Songs* (The Macmillan Company, New York), copyright by John A. Lomax and Alan Lomax, 1934: *The Wild Mizzourye, Foreman Young Monroe, The Erie Canal, Ground-Hog, The Old Grey Goose (Go Tell Aunt Nancy), Hush-You-Bye (All the Pretty Little Horses), Frog Went A-Courtin', Run, Boys, Run (Patterol), We're Gonna Raise a Rukus, Weevily Wheat, Billy Boy, Old Joe Clark, The Grey Goose, John Henry, The Ballad of the Boll Weevil, Stewball, The Roving Gambler, John Harty, The Midnight Special, Abdul, the Bul Bul Ameer, Fare-Thee-Well, O Honey (Dink's Song), Little Mohee, Rye Whiskey,* and *Birmingham Jail (Down in the Valley).*

From *Our Singing Country* (The Macmillan Company, New York), copyright by John A. Lomax and Alan Lomax, 1941: *The Ram of Derby, The Lazy Man, Old Blue, My Good Old Man, Will You Wear Red? (Jennie Jenkins), Lolly Toodum, Old Man's Courtship (Old Shoes and Leggin's), Cotton-Eye Joe, Hush, Little Baby, The Old '97, Wake up, Darlin' Corey, Pretty Polly, The Hammer Song (Take This Hammer), The Ox-Driving Song, Poor Boy, Brady and Duncan, The Rising Sun (The Rising Sun Blues),* and *Railroad Man (Lord, It's Almost Done).*

From *Cowboy Songs and Other Frontier Ballads* (The Macmillan Company, New York), copyright by John A. Lomax and Alan Lomax, 1938: *The Sioux Indians, Sweet Betsy from Pike, Jesse James, The Range of the Buffalo, The Old Chisholm Trail, Whoopie-Ti-Yi-Yo, The Dying Cowboy, The Zebra Dun,* and *My Government Claim.*

From *Negro Folk Songs as Sung by Leadbelly* (The Macmillan Company, New York), copyright by John A. Lomax and Alan Lomax, 1936; the songs republished in *Leadbelly* (Folkways Music Publishing, Inc., New York), copyright by Folkways Music Publishing, Inc., 1959: *Green Corn, Pick a Bale o' Cotton, Take a Whiff on Me (The Cocaine Song), Irene,* and *Alabama Bound.*

From *The Folk Songs of North America* (Cassell, London, and Doubleday and Company, Garden City, New York), copyright by Alan Lomax, 1960: *All Hid, Godamighty Drag,* and *What Month Was Jesus Born In?* (by Vera Hall, collected by R. P. Tartt).

From *Folk Song: U.S.A.* (Duell, Sloan & Pearce, New York), copyright by John A. Lomax and Alan Lomax, 1947; republished as *Best Loved American Folk Songs* (Grosset & Dunlap, New York), copyright by John A. Lomax and Alan Lomax, 1953: *The Bay of Mexico, Come All You Virginia Girls, Get Along Home, Cindy, Black-Eyed Susie.*

Collected and arranged by Alan Lomax, copyright by Penguin Books, Ltd (London), 1964: *Sourwood Mountain, The Cherry Tree Carol,* and *Delia.*

From *Songs of American Sailormen* (W. W. Norton, Inc., New York), copyright by Joanna Colcord, 1938: *The Stately Southerner, The Boston Come-All-Ye,* and *As I Walked down on Broadway.*

From *The American Songbag* (Harcourt, Brace & Company, New York), copyright by Carl Sandburg, 1927: *The Foggy Dew, Wanderin',* and *I'm A-Ridin' Old Paint.*

From *English Folk Songs of the Southern Appalachians* (in two volumes, Oxford University Press), copyright by Cecil Sharp and Maud Karpeles, 1932: *Pretty Saro* and *I Love My Love.*

Collected, arranged, and copyright by Frank Warner: *The Dying British Sergeant.*

Collected, arranged, and copyright by Ewan McColl: *Weary of the Railway.*

From *Favorite Songs and Play Party Games* (C. R. S., Delaware, Ohio), copyright by Jean Ritchie, 1940: *Goin' to Boston.*

Collected by Alan Lomax from the singing of Woody Guthrie; copyright by Woody Guthrie Estate, 1939: *Black Jack Davy (Gypsy Davy).*

Words and music by Woody Guthrie; copyright 1940, 1950, 1951; published by Folkways Music Publishing, Inc.: *So Long.*

A folk version as recorded by Jesse James for Decca Records; title copyright by Shapiro Bernstein (New York): *Casey Jones.*

Words and music by Kelly Pace; collected and arranged by John A. Lomax, 1939; copyright: *The Rock Island Line.*

Collected, arranged, and copyright by Ivan Walton: *The Little Brown Bull.*

Collected, adapted, and arranged by Horton Barker and Herbert Halpert: *The Farmer's Curst Wife.*

As sung by the Carter Family: *Worried Man* and *Single Girl.*

From *Sound Off* by E. A. Dolph (Farrar and Rinehart, New York); copyright 1929, 1942: *Goober Peas.*

Collected and arranged by Lee Hayes, published by Folkways Music Publishing Inc. (New York), 1951; copyright: *Follow the Drinkin' Gourd.*

Collected by Alan Lomax from the singing of Ella Mae Reese, the composer, 1937; copyright: *Which Side Are You On?*

INTRODUCTION

NORTH AMERICA has been the meeting place for a number of very diverse folksong styles, each one uprooted from its homeland and transported to the new world. These song families encountered one another in the wilderness of a raw, unsettled continent and were there subjected to myriad cultural influences, to violent and continuous social revolution, and to the unceasing movement of a great human host, migrating swiftly westward to the Pacific. Indeed, the special interest in the study of American folksong lies in the opportunity it affords one to observe a phenomenon which normally develops with glacial slowness, in the process of rapid evolution. Entire song stocks failed to survive the Atlantic crossing; others dwindled and died on the eastern shore; new families, sometimes derived from obscure and unimportant roots in the old world, flourished mightily in the new; certain medieval ballads spread across the whole country, side by side with new hybrid songs that altered with every decade. Recently, this verdant growth of rural melody has been exposed to the withering urban winds of the radio, record, and film industries, yet this new American country music quickly developed traits that appealed to city folk, so that a large body of living American folksong has won wide urban acceptance. In this fruitful combination of rural and urban influences, America resembles Spain, Cuba, and Brazil.

Every linguistic minority in the American melting pot has preserved at least some fragments of its oral tradition. For instance, those American Indian groups that managed to maintain their tribal and cultural identities still have their own songs and dances. In the Eastern states, Indian cultures were destroyed wholesale, but west of the Mississippi the larger tribes on reservations are now on the increase, and among them an Indian cultural renaissance is in progress. One hears of a phonograph company in Arizona that is manufacturing records of Indian songs and marketing them to the folk of the reservations. These Indians still sing and dance in ways that have been little affected by white contacts.* In the contrary direction – that is in the matter of the influence of Indian upon white folksong – there are only occasional if any traces.

The pressure of Americanization inclined the second generation immigrant to feel ashamed of the culture of his parents. Even so, exotic folkways survived in the U.S.A. to a surprising degree. In general, where a minority established a substantial geographic base and held to its original tongue, its folk music continued to be practised, and, in some cases, songs were kept alive that had passed

*A drastic change in policy under the Republican Administration reversed this trend; the tribes are being broken up, as the Indians are urged by the Bureau of Indian Affairs to sell their tribal lands, leave the reservations, and Americanize themselves.

out of currency in the country of origin. Further, new ballads, which reflected American experiences, were set to old tunes; and often the musicians who continued to play the traditional dances went on to make commercial recordings of 'pop' songs in every language and style, from Armenian to Turkish. On my song-hunting trips round the States I discovered that I could locate colonies of foreign-language speakers and singers by looking at the titles of the records in local juke boxes.

In Northern Michigan, for instance, I took down long passages of the Finnish epic, the *Kalevala*, from Finnish speaking miners, who were equally proud of their picket line ballads, born during the great copper mining strikes of the twenties. A Detroit beltline worker entertained me for an afternoon as he intoned Serbian epics of the Turkish wars to the accompaniment of his one-stringed *gusla*. Black-bearded patriarchs in the prosperous Amish colony in Indiana sang hymns for the recording machine in a style that had altered little since the Reformation. A valiant police captain, by the name of O'Neill, compiled the definitive collection of Irish harp, bagpipe, and fiddle tunes during his off-duty hours in Chicago. Hebridean waulking songs may still be heard in fine form along the Nova Scotia coast. Such a catalogue of American survivals of non-English folksong might be almost indefinitely extended.

As for the three largest linguistic minorities – the Germans of Southern Pennsylvania, the French of Eastern Canada and Louisiana, and the Mexicans of the Southwest – each of these groups has a lively folksong tradition. The French *voyageurs* paddled their way across the continent, singing folksongs that often surpass in beauty the finest antique ballads of France itself, while the Cajun rice farmers of southwestern Louisiana dance to the *fais-do-do*, a special family of tunes which are as tangy as the blues. The Spanish-speaking folk of the Southwest and Mexico still perform their medieval mystery plays, and they have created a body of topical ballads called *corridos*, which celebrate the feats of *vaqueros* and revolutionary leaders and detail local crimes of passion down to the final gout of blood.

Now we must pass on to a discussion of the song types to which this volume is limited – the folksongs in the English language which have been popular in America since colonial times.

The American frontier brought together families of Scots, Irish, Welsh, and English settlers from every part of Britain. The majority were labourers or artisans and, therefore, dialect speakers and carriers of their local folk traditions. In the new country linguistic and musical dialects were soon levelled off and absorbed into broad regional patterns that were novel and fructive amalgams of British folk speech and song. A man's accent counted for little in America. His neighbours judged him by his character, his talents, and his ability to adapt himself to the new modes of life and the folkways that were swiftly developing in the new continent.

Under these democratic conditions, songs and tunes were swapped between the different breeds of British colonials with a freedom and rapidity unknown in the old country. In the North the singing Irishman became the principal entertainer and song-maker; and in the South the Scots-Irish played the principal role. The frontier forcing-ground produced a composite (Scots-English-Irish-Welsh-German) musical style which has so shaped American song variants that it is often extremely difficult to determine in which regions of Britain they had their origin.

Speaking broadly, the white backwoodsman sang solo – or in poorly blended unison – with his body stiffly held and with little facial expression, in a uniform, hard, throaty, often high-pitched and nasal vocal style. He used decorated melodies which frequently conform to old gapped scales to mount songs in which the words and the plots mattered more than the tunes. This style did not lend itself easily to accompaniment or to singing in chords.

Within this generalized Anglo-American folksong style, varying ethnic and historical influences bred three main regional song families: the Yankee, the Southern poor white, and the cowboy. These three sub-styles share many themes, tunes, and patterns of preference, yet each has qualities which characterize most of the songs of a region.

Yankee singers preserved the older British lyric songs and ballads for a time, but soon replaced them with an extensive bunk-house literature of journalistic ballads in the eighteenth–nineteenth century 'come-all-ye' style. These new ballads dealt in factual terms with the adventures of soldiers, sailors, fishermen, and lumberjacks. Their tunes were largely Irish or Scots. (Section I.)

Meanwhile, the Southern mountains preserved the traditional British ballads, lyric songs, and dance tunes in comparative isolation for almost two hundred years, thus permitting the emergence of hybrid songs, which were on the one hand fusions of Scots, Irish, and English influences and, on the other, genuine reflections of pioneer culture patterns (Section II). This mountain music gradually came into stimulating competition with urban popular song and with an emerging Afro-American tradition, and there developed a large body of indigenous Southern white spirituals, lyric songs, and dance tunes.

Yankee and Southern backwoods singers met in the cow-camps of the far west and together composed the cowboy songs which partake of the qualities of both the earlier styles. The cowboy singer was a Yankee balladeer with a southern accent. (Section V.)

By far the most original songmakers to come to America, however, were the slaves from West Africa. In many parts of Latin America the Negroes continued to speak their native languages and to practise their pagan religions, but in the United States they became English-speaking, Protestant Americans, although at first of an inferior social status. In spite of this forced acculturation, hundreds of African words (e.g. 'pickaninny'), much African folklore (as in the Uncle Remus tales), and what might be termed a generalized African cultural bias did survive. (Nos. 39, 41, 42, 45, Section III.)

The musically well trained Negroes quickly picked up the main British tune and song types and learned to play European instruments. They absorbed European chordal patterns so rapidly that they were soon singing Protestant hymns in fine improvised harmony – while their white neighbours struggled to learn harmony from backwoods singing teachers. Even so, the slave's musical thinking remained basically African.

Like his brothers in Africa and Latin America, the American Negro preferred to sing in groups, using European harmonies in the African polyrhythmic style. He sang at normal speaking pitch, but played with his voice, introducing falsetto leaps, grunts, bass notes, etc. Deprived of his drum orchestras, he made drums of his hands, feet, thighs, and lips, and accompanied his songs with complex clapping and foot-tapping rhythms. The African leader-chorus pattern prevailed. Most melodies were brief, and texts often fragmentary. The demands of the dance or of other rhythmic activities dominated his strongly emotional and frankly erotic songs.

In its early stages, then, the map of English-language folksong in America may be viewed as an island of Afro-American polyrhythm and polyphony, surrounded by a sea of Anglo-American solo singing. Its third phase, which is still continuing, is a complex mingling of these two traditions – Negro music becoming less African, while white folksong is increasingly influenced by Negro style. The Anglo-Afro-American hybrid types, produced at various stages of culture contact, are the most distinctive of American songs.

The main body of collected American folksong consists of British survivals, or of the songs produced on the expanding frontier during the nineteenth and twentieth centuries. In this period, the changing demands and the hard necessities of pioneer life governed the survival of songs, whether traditional or newly minted. The typical pioneer was enamoured of the new, and impatient with tradition unless it had an American frontier flavour. He discarded non-essentials in folksongs as well as in technology. Your Davy Crockett, your cowboy, your rural Negro preacher, your mountain fiddler, your Negro levee camp singer was each aware of his own type; each savoured his own (sometimes fantastical) originality; each had strong opinions as to what constituted an appropriate song for his setting.

However, because these pioneers were hard-working, migratory, and essentially practical, with little leisure for creativity, they tended to retain from tradition whatever suited the basic *mores* and emotions of frontier life. Yet the home-made, make-do, hand-me-down patchwork of American pioneer culture never accepted British song traditions passively. It censored the songs that it found shocking. It discarded songs which had no new function in the wilderness. It clung hard to the old songs which conformed to its emotional predilections. A few brief examples will serve to illustrate these principles.

The ritual songs and dances (Morris dancing, May ceremonies, etc.) which were in full flower in seventeenth- and eighteenth-century Britain were never transplanted to America; of all this rich seasonal lore only a few carols have survived intact. (No. 54.) On the other hand, the popular and democratic British country dance bloomed again in the wilderness, combining elements from all parts of the United Kingdom. At first its complex patterns were simplified into two or three fundamental forms, which could be easily learnt by strangers meeting in a new place. The emergent American country dances centred round the caller or prompter, who organized and directed his heterogeneous crowd by chanting the figures of the dance. Unshackled by tradition, the caller felt free to mix his calls, and this freedom led to the continuous development of variant forms of the square dance and the running set, until they became as much identified with the American scene as cornbread and whiskey.

Mouth music (lilting), in which a singer takes the place of the fiddler or piper, seems to be a trait of the Celtic areas of Great Britain. In America one finds these verbalized instrumental melodies in Canada and in the whole South and Southwest. (Nos. 45–52.)

The old British sea shanty, which had fallen into disuse in the British Navy of the eighteenth century, roared into life again on American privateers, packets, and clippers. These ships were notoriously undermanned in proportion to the press of the sail they carried. Their efficiency and speed depended on the shanties, which spurred the men to incredible efforts at the sheets and halliards. For a period of almost fifty years the shanties lived mainly aboard American ships, often led by Negroes, and most authorities now agree that American seamen had a hand in creating or re-working a large number of the sailor work-songs we know today. (Nos. 8–10.)

An astonishing number of classical British ballads (over 100) have been discovered in America, more than have recently been found in oral currency in the British Isles. Here, however, the pioneer was ruthlessly selective and only those ballads survived in wide circulation which were comprehensible in American terms, or which conformed to American emotional patterns. For instance, the common Scots type, in which the girl is raped and then married by a stranger, is rare in the United States, while ballads dwelling upon the dire are known throughout the country. (No. 24.)

Historical ballads (*Chevy Chase*), tales of courtly intrigue (*The Death of Queen Jane*), ballads of supernatural beings (*Tam Lin*), all these occur rarely. In American versions noble protagonists generally lose their titles; British place names are altered, sometimes in very amusing ways. An American variant of *Lord Randall* begins

Where have you been, Willie Ransome, Willie Ransome,
Where have you been, my own darlin' one?
Been a-ramblin' an a-gamblin', mother, make my bed soon,
For I'm sick at the heart and I'd fancy lie down.

An American version of *Geordie* has it that

Charlie stole the king's white steeds
And sold them in Virginny . . .

Although the pioneer did thus radically prune and edit his heritage of medieval ballads, he was also culturally conservative. Having little besides his traditional songs to grace the hard life of the log-cabin and work camp, he abided by certain old songs with deep loyalty and affection. They were passed from hand to hand, from mother to child right across the continent. Such antiquities as *Edward, The Douglas Tragedy, The Golden Vanity, The Cruel Mother*, and many others have been found in oral circulation far more frequently in America than in Great Britain.

Barbara Allen, Lord Lovell, Lord Thomas and Fair Eleanor, The Frog's Courtship – the ballads whose themes found an echo in the *mores* of rural America – became completely at home there. On the whole, British survivals disappeared as the frontier moved west, but the songs that reached the Pacific Coast, though altered, are still recognizable. (Nos. 84, 85.) Certain very old ballads, such as *The Farmer's Curst Wife*, can still bring laughter and applause in city night clubs anywhere in the country. (No. 23.)

In the South, where isolation and illiteracy fostered the oral tradition, another strong trend is observable – the gradual breakdown of the ballad and its replacement by the lyric song. In the Southern mountains, in fact, all secular songs, lyric or narrative, were termed love (erotic) songs. They deal, almost exclusively, with the frustrations or the tragic (and usually violent) destinies of lovers. (Nos. 17, 24, 30, 31, 100.) One may suppose that such themes had great appeal for the subservient and exploited backwoods wife who was the main carrier of traditional folk songs of this type. This southern preference for lyric song culminated in modern hillbilly music which now rivals Tin Pan Alley in volume of output, while far surpassing it in sheer melancholy. (Nos. 30, 103, 107.)

Approximately half of America's indigenous folk songs are religious. The settlers were looking for a land where they might worship God according to their own lights, and they were deeply concerned with the problems of sin and individual salvation. In fact, discussions of religious questions long remained the chief intellectual diversion in rural America; and the American Revolution of 1776 was as much a popular rising against the established churches as against the King's Government. Once set free to sing and pray as they pleased, the pioneers created a literature of new and lively religious songs, which suited them far better than the psalms of the Puritans. The texts were often bookish verse, but the tunes were largely adaptations of secular folk songs and, as time went on, these white spirituals have become steadily more popular in character. (See Nos. 55, 56.) Today, the songs which make the white Holy Rollers dance in the aisles are almost indistinguishable from the liveliest Negro spirituals.

From the outset white and Negro spirituals exhibited striking and fundamental differences of style and content. While the rural whites sang with solemn face and rigidly held body in harsh, unblended unison, or with book-learnt chords, the Negroes blended their rich voices in improvised harmonies, swayed their bodies, clapped their hands, patted their feet – in sum, danced their hymns. These newly converted and deeply religious Africans, bowed down by the twin burdens of slavery and a Calvinistic conviction of original sin, poured into their spirituals the profound grief of the slave, and expressed in veiled, yet noble imagery their yearning for freedom or liberation in death. By the time of the Civil War, the Negro had created a body of religious folk-songs which matched in beauty the best of European hymnology. These spirituals, collected by the abolitionists and used by them to demonstrate that the Negro had a Christian soul and therefore deserved freedom, were the first American folk songs to be seriously studied. (Nos. 57–62.)

Much earlier, however, the slaves had made a great impression with their aptitude for the dance. In fact, the dances of the Negroes seemed so extraordinary and charming to the whites that even the sternest masters permitted their slaves to hold public dances on holidays. By the time of the American revolution, Negro fiddlers were frequently chosen to play for the most elegant Southern balls. They quickly absorbed the British country dance tradition and then went on to compose reels and jigs of their own, full of catchy African rhythms, yet sufficiently British to be easily learned by the white musicians. (Nos. 41, 42, 45.)

It was these Negro plantation reels that Dave Rice, Dan Emmett, and other white theatrical people imitated in their early black-face minstrel acts. Their pseudo-Negro songs enjoyed a tremendous vogue during the nineteenth century. There were scores of touring minstrel companies, that were the rage in Paris and played Royal Command performances in London. The influence of minstrel song appears in the sea shanty, in both British and American country dancing and in Negro song itself. (Nos. 44, 46.) The minstrel show finally opened the way for the talented Negro to enter the entertainment world. It led directly to the development of ragtime piano music and this, again, played an important part in the growth of jazz in New Orleans. In this gay, tolerant city, Negroes had an unparalleled opportunity to master European orchestral instruments. Their fashion of 'singing through

their horns' and their ability to improvise harmonically and rhythmically in concert, brought a new musical style into existence, which has deeply influenced the popular music of the whole world.

At first the instrumental equipment of Southern folk musicians was slight. The backwoodsman had home-made whistles, dulcimers (jaw harps, mouth bows), and fiddles upon which he played dance tunes or song airs. The Negroes had various simple rhythmic instruments such as the bones, and a primitive North African chordo-phone called the *banjar*, which Thomas Jefferson mentions as the principal instrument among Virginia Negroes in the 1760s. The three-string *banjar* became the four-and five-string banjo of the minstrels, and about the middle of the nineteenth century it began to penetrate the Southern mountains. Early home-made banjos had no frets and so did not impose conventional harmony upon the antique modal airs of the mountains. The silvery ringing tone of the banjo lent new colour to the old tunes, and its pinging strings provided an unobtrusive rhythmic counterpoint. These mountain songs accompanied on the five-string banjo represented an important development in the history of British folk music. They were very likely the first folk songs in this tradition since the days of the harpers to be accompanied by a stringed instrument, played in folk style; and they were probably the first *English-language* folk songs to have an appropriate style of self-accompaniment. (Nos. 30, 31, 33.)

These 'banjo songs', which very properly sound Oriental to most listeners, had a couple of generations to mature before Negro folk musicians, who had begun to tire of the banjo, brought the guitar into the mountains. At first both Negroes and whites played the guitar in banjo style, using few full chords, and as a result between 1890 and 1920, there arose a number of American guitar styles which are fully as interesting, though not as complex, as the ensemble playing of Latin America. Soon, however, the six conventional triads began to predominate and, bit by bit, the old modal airs were flattened out and made to conform to the tempered scale and to conventional European harmony. Instrumental combinations of fiddle, banjo, guitar, and mandolin were formed, which at first performed mountain square-dance tunes but, as the players gained confidence and prestige, created a whole new song literature for the poor whites of the South, the so-called hillbilly songs. This music has had a wide market on records and over the radio – since the first hillbilly record, issued with great reluctance by RCA Victor, sold half a million copies; it has been extensively commercialized; yet, at its core, it is folk. Its most expert performers are still unlearned musicians who play by ear and are constantly evolving unconventional sounds. Their string ensembles, the so-called Blue Grass bands, today rival in virtuosity the orchestras of the Balkans.

The catalytic agent in Southern folksong has always been the Negro singer. For him, song was not a specialized activity, requiring an effort of memory, undertaken with embarrassment and in conformity with rigid social canons. Song flowed easily from his throat while he worked, danced, or worshipped, and in the natural rhythms of these activities. Thus tunes changed their roles with chameleon-like facility, spirituals becoming worksongs, then being used for dances, then as lullabies. Nor did the Negro singer require long, subtle melodies for his enjoyment. He could amuse himself for an hour with a short phrase or two, repeating a line endlessly until it acquired the patina that came to white folksong only after generations of oral transmission. His full-blown songs were made up of these phrases, reshuffled and reworked with every performance, and passing, unremarked, from song to song, like so many pieces of coral that are strung and restrung. (Compare Nos. 42, 45, 46, 64, 65, 66.) A good Negro singer is a great improviser, and for him every performance of a song is a fresh act of creation; indeed, it is normal for a Negro folksinger to announce at the end of a song, 'This here song was composed by myself.' Naturally, such a singer is, by and large, impatient with old songs; every season, every important occasion, produces a fresh crop of variants, which may be forgotten as a fresh crop comes on.

A catalogue of the types of work songs the American Negro created as he toiled for his white masters would summarize the building of the South, for it was his handskills that carved the South of today out of the wilderness. He had a song for every job; there were even songs that matched the rhythm of card-playing, and others for heaving the lead on Mississippi steamboats! (Nos. 63–71.) These work songs expressed more directly than the spirituals the Negro's true feelings, his resentment of his lot and his ironic view of his masters. (Nos. 65, 68–70.) At the same time, the work songs were conservative, musically speaking – retaining more African traits than any other Negro song types. (Nos. 68–71.) A gang of prisoners chopping wood on a Mississippi prison farm today sounds, except for the language they use, as if it might have come from West Africa. The most exotic of all these work songs were the *hollers*, the long, wailing, rhythmic complaints of the Negro mule driver. These *hollers* gave rise to the *blues*.

Up until the 1890s, the Negro dance continued in its antebellum patterns, with lively square and step dancing which combined movements from white pioneer dances, from plantation reels and from the dances of the minstrel show. Around the turn of the century, however, a new type of dance became popular in the Mississippi Valley south of Memphis. As in the popular waltz, polka, and cakewalk, the couple danced in a face-to-face embrace, but in the Mississippi *slow drag*, *scrawnch*, etc., the embrace was intimate and the dancers moved with the frank sensuality of the *danse du ventre* of Africa, and the *Place Congo* of New Orleans.

This 'jazz' dancing was accompanied by a new kind of music called *the blues*. (Nos. 100–2.) Some unknown country Negro guitarist had learned to match the melodies of the levee camp singers along the Mississippi, and so there sprang up a school of guitar 'pickers' who could make a guitar talk – that is, speak the words of songs in Afro-American musical dialect. Thus the blues began, and this great dark river of song has flowed on ever since, producing America's unofficial national anthem (*The St Louis Blues*) and her most distinctive symphonic work (*The Rhapsody in Blue*), providing the distinctive colour for jazz (No. 101) and giving rise to tens of thousands of verses that reflect the loneliness and conflict of modern man in the west. The itinerant Negro labourer of the Mississippi Valley was the first of us to feel like 'a poor boy a long way from home', 'an engine without no driving wheel', but in the ensuing fifty years many of us have come to share this feeling and to accept the blues as the deep song of our epoch.

Like the first hillbilly records, the first blues were runaway hits (No. 101). The large, respectable gramophone companies soon forgot their musical snobbishness when this 'countrified caterwauling' proved to be good business. Field crews toured the south and recorded blues, ballads, spirituals, square-dance music, and hillbilly songs of every type. The records sold in volume to large sections of the submerged, virtually illiterate Southern working-class which never before had found an outlet for their art.

Broadcasting stations in the Southern states built their entire programming around hillbilly music; mountain guitar players became stars with a national following. A new branch of the burgeoning American entertainment industry with its own publishing houses, theatrical circuits, radio stations, and record companies catered to the national rural working-class demand for hillbilly music.

Unfortunately, racial prejudice and exploitation did not allow the same scope to Negroes during this period. Southern radio stations did not often put their local Negro folk artists on the air, and unscrupulous businessmen took advantage of the naïveté and timidity of talented Negro folk composers. For these and other reasons, Negro Southern blues singers tended to give up their art or to move North and seek for a paying audience in the folk population transplanted to certain Northern cities. Today one can find the best of folk blues performers in Chicago and Detroit, rather than in Memphis or Atlanta.

None the less, urban folk music is in a flourishing condition in America. On the one hand, the revival movement, motivated by collectors, scholars, teachers, and enthusiasts, has succeeded in turning a very large section of American youth into 'singers of folk songs'. On the other hand there are the professionals – the hillbilly bands, the blues singers, the Negro quartets and gospel singers – who find an expanding outlet through records, the radio, and now television. Much of *Rock and Roll* contains elements of gospel song, blues, and jazz. Its audience has grown accustomed to a folky 'pop' song sound, and this is one reason, certainly, why so many folk songs have recently appeared at the top of the hit parade, e.g. *Tom Dooley*, *Staggerlee*, *Day-O*, *The Roving Kind*, *Black-Eyed Susie*, among many others. Thus in America, as nowhere else in the world, the mass amusement industry, which certainly destroys the roots of folksong in the village, helps to foster it on regional and national levels. Discs and radio programmes replace the ballad sheet and the wandering minstrel.

Having thus briefly reviewed the social and institutional history of American folksong, it may be worth while now to summarize its most salient features. It is a hybrid of hybrids, the two main stocks being Anglo-Celtic and West African. On the one hand, it has preserved many old British tunes and modes of decorating these tunes; on the other, it has become more and more an accompanied, even orchestral song style, pervaded by a strong beat and hard driving rhythms absent in modern British folksong. Older Irish or Scottish types of ornamentation have tended to disappear or to be replaced by Negro slides and syncopations, 'blued' notes, etc.; and, owing again to Negro influence, the songs have become with every decade more polyphonic and polyrhythmic. Although African types of tunes and rhythms have survived, the Negro has, on the whole, accepted the common tune and song forms of his Southern white neighbours, while giving them an African treatment. He adopted our musical conventions, but retained his own musical habits.

The Afro-American hybrids which thus developed coloured the whole of modern American folksong and are now deeply affecting popular music everywhere. There can be no question about the source of the appeal of American music for the world audience: it is the most cosmopolitan of styles, representing the offspring of the marriage of two great musical families, the African and the European (as represented in the folksong of the British Isles). On the other hand, it is a thoroughly urbanized folk art, created by rural folk who were aware of city standards or by slum dwellers who had not forgotten their country origin. Thus its verses have great appeal to an urban audience. (Nos. 86–111.)

*

Few acknowledgements are necessary in this book except to my father, John A. Lomax. As a boy he grew up beside the Chisholm Trail in Texas, and the singing of the cowboys aroused in him a romantic interest in the ballad. Later, with the help of a fellowship from Harvard University, he carried out the first broadscale survey of native American song, ranging over the West and Southwest, collecting all the cowboy songs and many of the Negro songs that are universally known today. (Nos. 67, 73–82, 89–91, 93.) His first book, *Cowboy Songs*, published in 1910, aroused the interest of students in every part of America in this field, and stimulated the research which later produced many volumes of American regional ballads.

In 1933 I joined him in his new field work. Through the generosity of the Rockefeller and Carnegie Foundations, we were equipped with a portable electric disc recorder, and with this instrument we were able to document the full vocal and instrumental richness of American folksong performance. These recordings formed the basis of the Archive of American Folk Song at the Library of Congress in Washington. In the next decade, recording together and separately, we added more thousands of songs on discs to the Archive's collection. Publication of books and records, together with programmes on Columbia Broadcasting System, awakened national interest in America's living folksong tradition. Today the singers and the songs we found and presented in those years have become the focus of a folksong revival, in which hundreds of full-time singers and researchers are employed and a sizable fraction of American youth have become involved. In New York City, for instance, where there were in 1933 only a handful of five-string banjo players, there are several thousand.

With the few noted exceptions, therefore, the songs that make up this volume of the standard American folksongs were discovered and shaped by my father and myself. Their selection has been no easy task. Within the limits of a small volume I have tried to present all types of songs and to include some unfamiliar songs, as well as many of the favourites. Songs as well known as *Home on the Range*, or *Swing Low Sweet Chariot*, were assumed to be common property. If I have leaned in any direction, it is towards the songs which were the favourites of the recent British folksong movement, the so-called 'skiffle' singers, who preferred our American hybrids to their own traditions.

I have resung all the melodies so as to make them easier for the person inexperienced in folksong. The vocal decorations used by folk singers are extremely difficult to notate, and just as hard to read when notated. The only way they can be learnt is by listening to records and imitating what the singers do. This will prove a most rewarding experience, and in fact it is the only way to turn an urban singer into a good ballad singer. I suggest that every singer study the records listed in Appendix 1.

The final difficulty is the metre, which is extremely free and variable. The folk singer knows how to stretch or collapse his tunes, to vary his rhythm slightly, to dwell upon a note or shorten it so that every word in the line is clearly heard and the ever-changing meter of the folk balladist can be accommodated. This is a skill which comes only with practice.

The following suggestions may help the novice. (1) In Negro songs, establish a strong, swinging rhythm and hold to it, eliding or swallowing extra syllables where necessary. (2) In white songs, especially of the lyric or narrative type, let the metre of the verse dominate the musical rhythm; sing each line on its own and introduce holds or pauses where necessary. (3) Negro songs should be sung expressively with full voice and plenty of body movement. (4) White songs should be sung with little facial or vocal expression and in a flat, even, somewhat nasal tone.

Appendix I gives a brief method for accompanying American folksongs on guitar. The proper guitar chords for the songs are indicated in letters above the melody line of each song. In this aspect of the work, and in noting down the tunes, I have been assisted by Peggy Seeger, one of the most talented singers and arrangers of American folk songs.

Elizabeth Poston's piano settings seem to me models of their kind. They assist the songs, without obtruding themselves. They reflect the authentic banjo, guitar, and Negro piano accompaniments she has studied, yet retain their own pianistic integrity. When the pianist has played through these accompaniments and absorbed the many ingenious devices Miss Poston has worked out, he will be prepared to go on and improvise his own settings of other songs of the same types. Above all, he should use the framework she has provided, but feel free to adapt the piano to the changing meters of the songs.

Final thanks are due to Shirley Collins, who has assisted in the whole work of preparing the manuscript for publication.

ALAN LOMAX

NOTE ON THE SONG SETTINGS

THESE settings are not just an arranger's fancy: they have been based in the idiom of the American folk musicians, transmuted into terms of practical piano playing from the folk singers' and players' original styles. These need to be heard and studied for realization of their full beauty and effect. In spite of the fun and stimulus we owe to the best of Tin Pan Alley, the accretions of commercialized, arranged American song are far indeed from the music of the native folk singer. He it is, in his sincerity and natural artistry, who has been studied here, and his music reproduced in models to serve, at least, as accessible representations of the social documentary of a great nation in its folk music. The difference between setting folk songs of a purely vocal origin (e.g. the Southern Mountain songs of British derivation, such as *The Cherry Tree Carol, Pretty Saro*) and those with an instrumental tradition (e.g. *Uncle Reuben, Green Corn, Pick a Bale o' Cotton*) is very marked. There are thus striking divergences between the British folksong tradition and that of America, in which, though the strains meet and mingle, instrumental accompaniment is still a basic, living force.

These piano accompaniments, therefore, where they cannot exactly reproduce the accompaniments of the American folk singers, aim at approximation and at providing a practical basis for performance not beyond moderate technical ability. Anyone acquainted with the astounding technique of the finest American folk players, and the exciting rhythmical complexities with which they can quite naturally accompany a simple melody upon guitar or banjo, will realize that the original treatment cannot always, short of virtuosity, be applied to the piano – just as it is not possible to write down certain blues effects. But with understanding and ingenuity, permitting some reservations and simplifications, it is possible in a considerable measure to communicate faithfully the spirit and to reproduce styles – to catch the essential, as Bartók did with Hungarian folksong, Falla with Spanish. To this end, the resources of modern piano playing are enlisted, with comprehensive use of the pedals, imaginative approach to light and shade, the contrasts of freedom and strict rhythm, and of clean playing and impressionistic blurring which may occur within one song (e.g. *Blue-Tail Fly, Frankie and Johnny*).

A few practical notes on principles and treatment may be found helpful.

Metronome indications are given as a basic guide, subject to the variations of mood and inclination in spontaneous folk singing. The simple guitar harmonies given above the stave do not always match those of the piano part.

Pedalling, though its use or absence is specifically marked here and there (e.g. in Nos. 56, 89, 95), is assumed throughout. It is important that in songs based on guitar accompaniments, e.g. No. 33, *Wake Up, Darlin' Corey*, in which the guitar's characteristics of quick thrumming and of overtones imitated by pedalling are essential to the song's urgency and atmosphere, or the quick, light figuration characteristic of guitar and five-stringed banjo, as in No. 27, *My Good Old Man*, No. 30, *Single Girl*, and No. 50, *Get Along Home, Cindy*, the style should be treated imaginatively as such in the piano versions.

There is a strong difference between the treatment of the energetic, unsubtle honky-tonk style of early rhythm-piano of such songs as No. 46, *We're Gonna Raise a Rukus*, and the sensitive, sensuous idiom of southern blues, in which 'blue' notes, the purposeful ambiguities of major/minor, deliberately softened outlines, and the contrasts of indefinite with definite (e.g. dry 'walking bass'), need to be assimilated and sympathetically realized. In instances where quarter-tone notes are indicated specifically (these are notes with an interval smaller than a semitone, in which the singer lazes between two half-tones) an accompaniment of non-committal harmony is provided to ease the singer's path and help to achieve an authentic effect. (No. 90.)

In contrast, the Western songs, known generally, if they are known at all, in versions that are saccharine imitations of the originals, are of a harmonic simplicity whose conviction and sincerity are rooted in primary chords – whether in the fiercely vital *Ox-Driving Song* (No. 74) or the gently insistent tonic-and-dominant repetition of *Whoopie-Ti-Yi-Yo* (No. 79) and *I'm a-Ridin' Old Paint* (No. 81), characteristic of the lone rider's nostalgic melancholy. Indeed, it is necessary to remember that this harmony, which is not the debased hybrid of popular exploitation but the unsophisticated usage of this particular American folk idiom, though it may sound oversimplified to undiscerning ears, is a genuine style. A diversity is here to be explored – humorous, pathetic, tender, virile. These settings were made to be enjoyed; it is hoped that the exploration will lead infectiously to the creative revelation, as well as to a revaluation, of a national literature of 'fine songs for singing'.

ELIZABETH POSTON

NOTE ON THE VOICE PART

THE vocal line given is for the first verse. In certain songs the fitting of the words of the remaining verses to the music is not straightforward owing to the different number of syllables in corresponding lines of verse. In these cases the notes to be sung in the second verse where they differ from the first have been added in small type, and act as a guide to the treatment of the remaining verses.

I
Yankee Songs

I. YANKEE SONGS

In colonial days New England probably had as rich a stock of folk music as the Southern mountains. Collectors have recently discovered old ballads, folk hymns, fiddle tunes, local narratives and ditties all the way from the green woods of Maine to the blue Allegheny hills. But New England did not long provide the stable, isolated, integrated rural society that is the normal requirement for the growth of folksong. Twenty-five years of war with the Indians and the British, the continual movement of population into the region and on to the west, the rise of industry and of bookish, pragmatic, cosmopolitan Yankee culture favoured the rise of literature, not folk ballads.

The ubiquitous Yankee did his singing on the windy decks of the packet ships with which he conquered the trade of the world. When he tackled the evergreen forests that reached from Maine to Minnesota, he took his fo'c'sle ballads with him. Singing for a bunk-house audience of brawny Irish and Scots timber tigers, he made over the narratives of sea-adventures into tales of death and danger in the woods and on the river drives. These same tunes, dressed anew in buckskin or wearing chaps and a ten-gallon hat, later crossed the plains with the forty-niners and rode night guard round longhorn herds in the Far West. Thus, although few of the folk songs of New England have lasted and become widely sung, and although this area developed no distinctive musical style of its own, it fed the Midwest and Far West with tunes and song ideas, and became the true grandparent of folk song there.

Folk singing in the North was solo, except in the shanties where the crew joined in on the refrains. On shipboard the valued singer was the man who knew the proper shanty for the job. He needed a strong voice to carry over the multitudinous noises of a vessel under way in a lively sea. He wanted a good memory and the wit to supply new lines when the situation required them. The men pulled all the better when a verse excoriated the mate or the captain, or when the shanty-leader reminded them of the girls they had left behind in port.

The same practical approach determined the character of the ballads of the sea and the woods. These horny-handed sons of toil had no great appetite for fantasy or lyric nuance. Their daily lives and their adventures and hardships were fantastic enough. They enjoyed listening to long, factual come-all-ye's which told the stories of hard voyages and industrial accidents. Men like themselves played the central roles in these songs, and were mourned by their admiring comrades. These pioneer workmen praised a song by saying, 'That's just exactly how it happened', or 'that there song is as true as steel'.

Although a good voice was by no means rare among them, it was not essential to the come-all-ye singer. He might not carry the tune but his voice must be loud and clear; he had to know the words and 'speak them out plain' and not falter until the whole story had been told. Often he spoke the last half-line to signify he had come to the end of the ballad, as is still the practice in some parts of Ireland today. Indeed, from very early days until the present, the singing Irishman has been the principal singer and song-maker in the north.

This Yankee tradition of realistic ballads, in which the workman played the hero's part, was leavened by the Yankee fondness for dry humour. 'Americans', Josh Billings remarked, 'luv caustic things; they would prefer turpentine to cologne water, if they had to drink either. So with the relish of humour; they must have it on the halfshell with cayenne.' Thus the story of marrying Captain Plowjigger of Maine. He had just buried his fourth wife when a friend, who had not heard of his loss, asked him how his wife was. 'Waal, to tell you the truth,' said the vigorous old Captain, 'I'm kinder out of wives just now.'

1. THE PIZEN SARPINT

Moderate ♩=86

1. In Spring-field moun-tain there did dwe-i-ell A love-ly youth I knew full we-i-ell.
CHORUS: Ri-tu-ri-nu, ri-tu-di-nay, Ri-tu-di-nu, ri-tu-di-nay.____

Guitarists may capo up one fret and play the chords in brackets

1 In Springfield mountain there did dwe-i-ell
A lovely youth I knew full we-i-ell.
Ri-tu-ri-nu, ri-tu-di-nay,
Ri-tu-di-nu, ri-tu-di-nay.

2 One day this youth did chance to go-i-o,
Down in the meadow for to mow-i-o. *(Chorus)*

3 He skeerst had mowed half round the fie-i-ield,
When a pizen sarpint tuck him by the he-i-eel. *(Chorus)*

4 He laid right down upon the grou-ow-ound,
Shut both his eyes and looked all ar-ow-ow-ound. *(Chorus)*

5 'O pappy da-wa-wad, go tell my ga-wa-wal,
That I'm goin' fer to die, I know I sha-wa-wal'. *(Chorus)*

6 'O John, O John, why did you go-wo-wo
Out in the meadow for to mo-wo-wow?' *(Chorus)*

7 'O Sal, O Sal, why don't you kno-wo-wow
When the grass gits ripe, it must be mo-wo-wowed?' *(Chorus)*

8 Sal tuck his heel all in her mou-ow-wouth,
And tried to suck the pizen ou-ow-wout. *(Chorus)*

9 But Sal she had a rotten too-oo-ooth,
And so the pizen kilt them bo-o-ooth. *(Chorus)*

10 Come all young girls and shed one tear-weer-weer,
For these young folks who died right here-weer-weer. *(Chorus)*

11 Come all young men and warnin' ta-wa-wake,
Don't never get bit by a rattle-sna-wa-wake. *(Chorus)*

America's first indigenous folk ballad concerns Timothy Myrick of Springfield, Massachusetts, who was bitten by a rattlesnake and died of the effects on 7 August 1761. A local poet composed a serious elegiac ballad about the incident, which struck the funnybone of the Yankees and was lampooned and spread in this comic form, first via the music-hall, later by word of mouth and in many variants, to every part of America.

2. THE DYING BRITISH SERGEANT

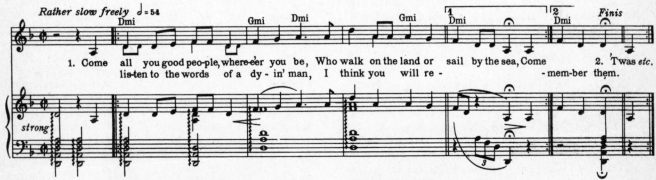

Rather slow freely ♩=54

1. Come all you good peo-ple, where-e'er you be, Who walk on the land or sail by the sea, Come lis-ten to the words of a dy-in' man, I think you will re- -mem-ber them. 2. 'Twas *etc.*

strong

1 Come all you good people, where-e'er you be,
Who walk on the land or sail by the sea,
Come listen to the words of a dyin' man,
I think you will remember them.

2 'Twas in October, the eighteenth day,
Our ship set sail for Amerikay,
The drums and the trumpets loud did sound,
And then to Boston we were bound.

3 And when to Boston we did come
We thought by the aid of our British guns
To make them Yankees own our King,
And daily tribute to him bring.

4 But to our sad and sore surprise
We saw men like grasshoppers rise,
'Freedom or death' was all their cry,
Indeed, they were not feared to die.

5 When I received my deathly wound
I bid farewell to England's ground,
My wife and children shall mourn for me
Whilst I lie dead in Amerikee.

A propaganda ballad from the American Revolutionary War, this come-all-ye purports to record the last words of a British redcoat who wished he'd stayed at home. Frank Warner recorded it in the 1940s from a New York State lumberjack, known as Yankee John Galusha, who growled and thundered it out as if the Hessians were still camped along the Hudson.

3. YANKEE DOODLE

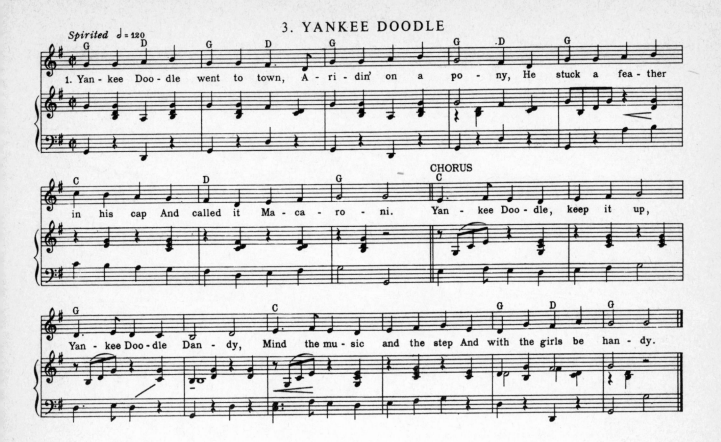

Spirited ♩ = 120

1. Yan-kee Doo-dle went to town, A-ri-din' on a po-ny, He stuck a fea-ther in his cap And called it Ma-ca-ro-ni.

CHORUS

Yan-kee Doo-dle, keep it up, Yan-kee Doo-dle Dan-dy, Mind the mu-sic and the step And with the girls be han-dy.

1 Yankee Doodle went to town,
   A-ridin' on a pony,
   He stuck a feather in his cap
   And called it Macaroni.
       Yankee Doodle, keep it up,
       Yankee Doodle Dandy,
       Mind the music and the step
       And with the girls be handy.

2 Father and I went down to camp,
   Along with Captain Gooding,
   And there we saw the men and boys
   As thick as hasty pudding. *(Chorus)*

3 There was Captain Washington
   Upon a slapping stallion,
   A-giving orders to his men,
   I guess it was a million. *(Chorus)*

4 The troopers they would gallop up,
   And fire right in our faces,
   It scared me almost half to death
   To see them run such races. *(Chorus)*

5 We saw a little barrel, too,
   The heads were made of leather,
   They knocked on it with little clubs
   And called the folks together. *(Chorus)*

6 And then we saw a giant gun
   Large as a log of maple,
   Upon a deuced little cart
   A load for father's cattle. *(Chorus)*

7 And every time they shoot it off
   It takes a horn of powder,
   It makes a noise like father's gun,
   Only a nation louder. *(Chorus)*

8 I can't tell you half I see,
   They kept up such a smother,
   So I took my hat off, made a bow
   And scampered home to mother. *(Chorus)*

9 Yankee Doodle is the tune,
   Americans delight in,
   'Twill do to whistle, sing or play
   And just the thing for fightin'. *(Chorus)*

British redcoats first sang *Yankee Doodle* as a satire upon the bumpkin American militia they defeated in the early battles of the American Revolutionary War. Later on, as one British soldier wrote, 'After the affair at Bunker's Hill, the Americans glory in it. *Yankee Doodle* is now their paean, played in their army, esteemed as warlike as *The Grenadiers' March*. It has become the lovers' spell, the nurses' lullabye. After our rapid successes it was not a little mortifying to hear them play this tune when their army marched down to our surrender.' In fact American fifes and drums played two tunes when Cornwallis surrendered his sword at Yorktown – *The World Turned Upside Down* and *Yankee Doodle*. The latter became an unofficial national anthem, the theme tune for American overseas radio in the Second World War, and a nursery song on both sides of the Atlantic. Despite much research, the origin of the melody has never been precisely determined – whether Dutch, French, Spanish, or Scots.

4. THE RAM OF DERBY

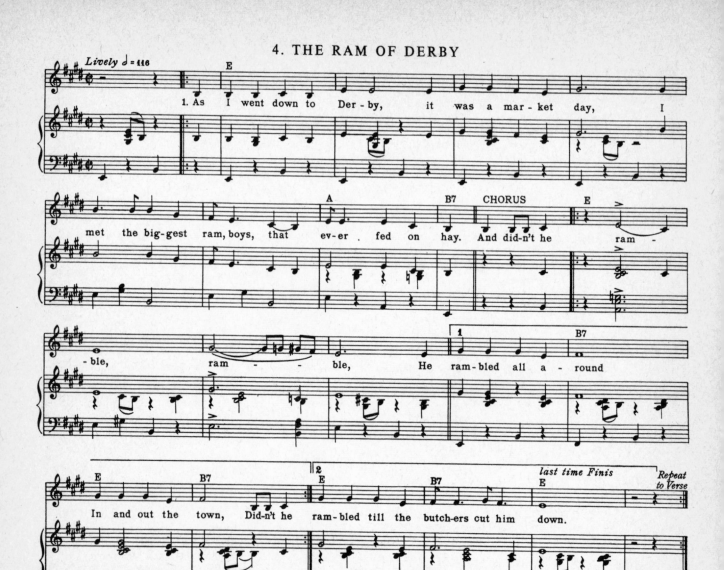

1 **As I went down to Derby, it was a market day,**
  I met the biggest ram, boys, that ever fed on hay.
    And didn't he ramble, ramble,
    He rambled all around,
    In and out the town,
    Didn't he ramble, ramble,
    He rambled till the butchers cut him down.

2 The hair upon this ram's back, it grew up to the sky,
  The eagles built their nests there, and the young ones dasn't fly.

3 The horns upon this ram's head, they grew up to the moon,
  A boy clumb up in January and didn't get down till June.

4 This ram he had a tail, it reached way down in hell,
  And every time he waggled that tail, he rung that hotel bell.

5 The hair on this ram's belly, it retch down to the ground,
  The devil stole a strand of that hair and made his wife a gown.

6 He rambled on the waterside, he rambled on the land,
  But when he went to the butcher's pen, 'twas there he met a man.

7 The man that butchered this ram was scairt of his life,
  He sent to Philadelphy to get him a four-foot knife.

8 The man that butchered this ram, sir, was drowned in the blood,
  And the boy that held the basin was washed away in the flood.

9 Took all the boys in our town to roll away his bones,
  Took all the girls in our town to roll away the stones.

10 The man that owned this ram, sir, he was awful rich,
  And the man who told the story was a lying sonofagun.

The Ram of Derby is said to have been the one song that President George Washington really liked to sing. This British tall tale was universally popular among American soldiers, sailors, and frontiersmen, acquiring among Negro singers the 'didn't he ramble' chorus, and becoming a rowdy, pagan funeral march for New Orleans jazz bands. I found this version in Michigan in 1938.

5. THE STATELY SOUTHERNER

1 It was the Stately Southerner that carried the Stripes and Stars,
  The whistling wind from west-nor'-west blew through her pitch-pine spars,
  With her starboard tacks aboard, my boys, she hung up to the gale,
  'Twas an autumn night, we raised the light on the Head of old Kinsale.

2 It was a clear and cloudless night; the wind blew steady and strong,
  As gaily over the sparkling deep our good ship bowled along,
  With the fiery foam beneath her bows the white wave she did spread,
  And bending alow her bosom in snow, she buried her lee cathead.

3 There was no talk of short'ning sail by him who walked the poop,
  And 'neath the press of her ponderous jib the boom bent like a hoop,
  And the groaning waterways told the strain that held her stout main-tack,
  But he only laughed as he gazed abaft at the white and glist'ning tack.

4 What looms upon our starboard bow, what hangs upon the breeze?
  'Tis time our good ship hauled her wind, we're abreast the old Saltees,
  For by her ponderous press of sail and by her stunted spars,
  We saw that our morning visitor was a British man-o'-war.

5 Up spake our noble Captain then, as a shot ahead of us passed,
  'Haul snug your flowing courses, lay your topsails to the mast.'
  Those Englishmen gave three loud hurrahs from the deck of their covered ark,
  And we answered back by a solid broadside from the deck of our patriot bark.

6 'Out booms, out booms,' our skipper cried. 'Out booms and give her sheet,'
  For the swiftest keel that ever was launched in all of the British fleet
  Came bearing down upon us, with the white foam at her bow,
  'Out booms, out booms, and give her sheet, spare not your canvas now.'

7 But a swifter keel was 'neath our feet, nor did our sea-boys dread
  When a star-spangled banner was hoisted, to the mizzen-peak was spread,
  And amid a thundering shower of shot with the stunsails hoisting away,
  Down the North Channel Paul Jones did steer just at the break of day.

Swift American privateers, captained by daredevil Yankee commanders, played an important part in winning the Revolutionary War. The Scots-American captain, John Paul Jones, snatched prizes from beneath the noses of British men-of-war all round the coasts of England; and this rousing sea-ballad commemorates one of his forays into the Irish Sea in 1778. In later years the song became a favourite of British as well as American seamen.

25

6. THE BOSTON COME-ALL-YE

With a hearty swing ♩.=88

1. 'Tis ad-ver-tised in Bos-ton, New York, and Buf-fa-lo,___ Five hun-dred brave A-me-ri-cans a-wha-ling for to go,___ Sing-ing, blow ye winds in the mo-orn-ing,___ Blow ye winds, hi-ho, Heave a-way your run-ning gear And blow, blow, blow___ 2. They etc.

1 'Tis advertised in Boston, New York, and Buffalo,
Five hundred brave Americans a-whaling for to go,
    Singing, blow ye winds in the mo-orning,
    Blow ye winds, hi-ho,
    Heave away your running gear
    And blow, blow, blow.

2 They tell you of the clipper ships, a-going in and out,
They say you'll take five hundred sperm before you're six months out.
    (Chorus)

3 It's now we're out to sea, my boys, the winds begin to blow,
One half the watch is sick on deck, the other half below.
    (Chorus)

4 Then comes the running rigging, which you're supposed to know,
It's 'Lay aloft, you sonofagun, or overboard you'll go.'
    (Chorus)

5 The skipper's on the quarterdeck, a-squintin' at the sails,
When up aloft the lookout sights a helluva school of whales.
    (Chorus)

6 'So clear away the boats, me boys, and after them we'll travel,
But if you get too near his flukes, he'll kick you to the devil.'
    (Chorus)

7 Now we've got him turned up and towing alongside,
We over with our blubberhooks and rob him of his hide.
    (Chorus)

8 Next comes the stowing down, me lads, it takes both night and day,
And you'll all get fifty cents apiece on the 190th lay.*
    (Chorus)

9 And when the ship is full of oil and we don't give a damn,
We'll bend on all our stu'nsails and head for Yankeeland.
    (Chorus)

10 When we get home, our ship made fast, and we are through our sailing,
    A winding glass around we'll pass and damn this blubber-whaling.
        (Chorus)

*Share.

This whaling ballad, set to an old English air, gives the deckhand's view of life on a New England whaler.

26

7. LITTLE MOHEE/OLD SMOKEY

Smooth and flowing ♩. = 66

1. As I was a-walk-in'_____ All by the sea-shore, The wind it did whis-tle,_____ The wa-ter did roar. 2. As etc. grove.

Repeats | *Finis*

LITTLE MOHEE

1 As I was a-walkin'
All by the seashore,
The wind it did whistle,
The water did roar.

2 As I sat amusin'
Myself on the grass,
Whom should I spy but a
Young Indian lass.

3 She sat down beside me,
Took hold of my hand,
Saying, 'You are a stranger
And in a strange land.

4 'But if you will follow,
You're welcome to come,
And dwell in the cottage
That I call my home.'

5 The sun was fast sinkin'
Far over the sea,
As I wandered along with
The lassie Mohee.

6 She asked me to marry,
And offered her hand
Saying, 'Father's the chieftain
All over this land.'

7 'O no, my dear maiden
That never can be,
I have a dear sweetheart
In my own countree.

8 'I will not forsake her,
I know she loves me,
Her heart is as true
As any Mohee.'

9 The last time I saw her,
She knelt on the sand,
And as my boat passed her
She waved me her hand.

10 But when I had landed
No one could I see
That did really compare
With the lassie Mohee.

11 The girl I had trusted
Proved untrue to me,
So I'll turn back my courses
Far over the sea.

12 I'll turn back my courses
And backward I'll rove,
I'll dwell with my Mohee
In the cocoanut grove.

OLD SMOKEY

1 On top of old Smokey,
All covered in snow,
I lost my true lover
From courtin' too slow.

2 For meetin' is pleasure
And partin' is grief,
And a false-hearted true-love
Is worse than a thief.

3 A thief he'll but rob you
And take what you have,
But a false-hearted true love
Will send you to your grave.

4 Your grave will decay you
And turn you to dust,
Not one boy in fifty
That a poor girl can trust.

5 They'll hug you and kiss you,
They'll tell you more lies,
Than crossties on a railroad
Or stars in the skies.

6 Just as sure as the dew falls
All on the green corn,
Last night he was with me,
This mornin' he's gone.

The original British come-all-ye is a rather pedestrian tale of the adventures of a British whalerman with a Polynesian girl on the island of Maui; but in America, where plenty of frontiersmen married Indians, the fair Kanaka was turned into a pretty Mohee or Mohican Indian. *Old Smokey*, the lament of the backwoods maiden deserted by her bold wagoner sweetheart, runs to the same tune as *Little Mohee*.

8. THE WILD MIZZOURYE

Guitarists may capo up two frets and play the D chords...D...G (Bmi)...D (F#mi)...A7...G (Bmi), etc.

1 O Shenandoah, I love your daughter,
  Away, you rolling river,
  O Shenandoah, I love your daughter,
  Away I'm bound to go, 'cross the wild Mizzourye.

2 A white man loved an Indian maiden, *etc.*
  With notions his canoe was laden, *etc.*

3 For seven long years he courted Sally, *etc.*
  For seven more he longed to have her, *etc.*

4 Farewell, my dear, I'm bound to leave you, *etc.*
  O Shenandoah, I'll not deceive you, *etc.*

5 A drinkin' rum and chawin' terbaccer, *etc.*
  A drinkin' rum and chawin' terbaccer, *etc.*

It is said that this song originated among the *voyageurs* – the fur traders who plied the Missouri rivers in their canoes and flatboats. The U.S. Cavalry, which came into its own fighting Indians in the same region, claims the song.

However, it is best known in its blue water version, sung as a capstan shanty by both British and American seamen.

9. AS I WALKED DOWN ON BROADWAY

1 As I walked down on Broadway,
  One evening in July,
  I met a maid who asked my trade.
  'A sailor John,' says I.
    And away, you Santee,
    My dear Annie,
    O you New York gals,
    Can't you dance the polka?

2 To Tiffany's I took her,
  I did not mind expense,
  I brought her two gold ear-rings,
  They cost me fifty cents. *(Chorus)*

3 Says she, 'You limejuice sailor,
  Now see me home you may.'
  But when we reached her cottage door
  She unto me did say: *(Chorus)*

4 'My flashman, he's a Yankee,
  With his hair cut short behind,
  He wears a tarry jumper
  And he sails in the Black Ball Line.' *(Chorus)*

Although singing at the capstan and the ropes had been practised aboard British ships for centuries, the great period of the shanties came after 1800 on the American packets and clippers. It is now generally believed that a sizeable proportion of the best and most familiar shanties are American, or at least Anglo-American, in origin. Such a one, evidently, is this capstan song from the swift Black Ball packets which broke all records on their runs between Liverpool and New York in the early 1800s.

10. THE BAY OF MEXICO

Moderate, strong and sweeping ♩ = 72

1. Nas-sau gals ain't got no combs, Hey - o, Su - zi-an-nah, They comb their heads with whip-per back-bones, Round the Bay of Mex-i - co.

CHORUS

Round that Bay of Mex-i - co, Hey - o, Su - zi-an-nah, O Mex-i - co is the place I be-long in, Round the Bay of Mex-i - co.

1 Nassau gals ain't got no combs,
  Hey-o, Suziannah,
  They comb their heads with whipper-backbones,
  Round the Bay of Mexico.

  Round that Bay of Mexico,
  Hey-o, Suziannah.
  O Mexico is the place I belong in,
  Round the Bay of Mexico.

2 When I was a young man in my prime,
  Hey-o, Suziannah,
  I took them young gals two at a time,
  Round the Bay of Mexico. *(Chorus)*

3 The reason those pretty gals love me so,
  Hey-o, Suziannah,
  'Cause I don't talk everything that I know,
  Round the Bay of Mexico. *(Chorus)*

All authorities on the sea shanty agree that American Negroes made a major contribution to the shanty repertoire during the nineteenth century. Scores of shanties are clearly Negro in origin; others, like this modern Bahaman version of the older *Santyana*, are Negro adaptations. (Recorded by Alan Lomax in Nassau in 1936.)

11. FOREMAN YOUNG MONROE

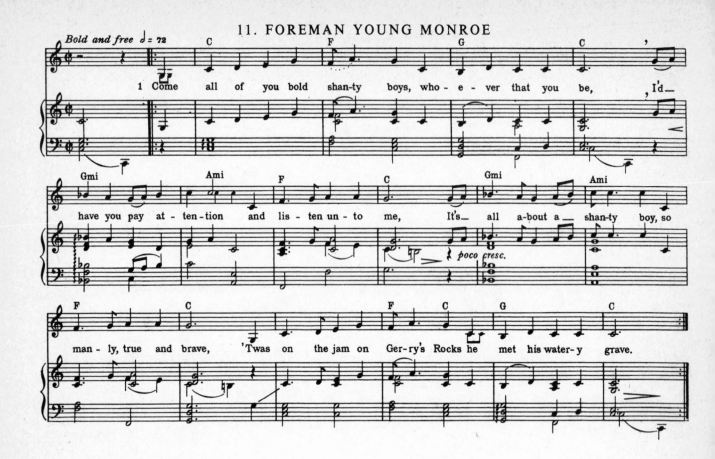

1 Come all of you bold shanty boys, whoever that you be,
   I'd have you pay attention and listen unto me,
   It's all about a shanty boy, so manly, true and brave,
   'Twas on the jam on Gerry's Rocks he met his watery grave.

2 It was on one Sunday morning, as you shall quickly hear,
   The logs was piled up mountains high, we could not keep them clear,
   But six of our Canadian boys did volunteer to go
   And break the jam on Gerry's Rocks with their foreman, Young Monroe.

3 They had not pulled off many logs until the boss did say,
   'I'd have you boys be on your guard, for the jam may soon give way,'
   He had no more than spoke these words, when the jam did break and go,
   And carried away those six brave youths with their foreman,
      Young Monroe.

4 They took him from the water, smoothed back his wavery hair,
   There was one fair form among them whose cries did rend the air,
   There was one fair form among them, a maid from Saginaw town,
   Whose screams and cries did rend the skies for her lover
      that was drowned.

5 Miss Clara was a noble girl, likewise a raftsman's friend,
   Her mother was a widow down by the river bend,
   The wages of her own true love the boss to her did pay,
   And liberal subscriptions from all the boys that day.

6 Miss Clara did not long survive her misery and grief,
   In less than three weeks afterwards death came to her relief,
   Twas scarcely three weeks afterwards that she was called to go
   And her last request was to be laid by her lover, Young Monroe.

7 Come all you brave young shantyboys, I'd have you call and see
   Two green graves by the river side where grows the hemlock tree,
   The shanty boys have marked the tree where lie those lovers low,
   (Spoken) With the name, the fate, the drownding date of the foreman, Young Monroe.

The Canadian and American lumberjacks, who worked in the great wilderness of conifers in the Northeast and round the Lake States, were great singers and ballad-makers in the come-all-ye tradition. Their ballad style laid the basis for the later cowboy songs, but their own adventurous lives in the lumberwoods and rafting the logs downstream on the Spring freshets, produced many fine ballads, the best loved of which is this realistic, yet sentimental tale.

12. THE ERIE CANAL

1. We were for - ty miles from Al - ba-ny, for - get it I ne-ver shall, What a ter-ri-ble storm we had one night on the
load-ed down with bar-ley, we were all of us full of rye, And the Cap - tain he looked down on me with a

E - RI-E Ca-nal; We were
dog-gone wick- ed eye.

CHORUS

O the E - RI-E's a - ris-in' and the whiskey's get-tin' low, And I
hard-ly think we'll get a drink, Till we get to Buf-fa-lo-o-o, Till we get to Buf - fa - lo.

1 We were forty, miles from Albany, forget it I never shall,
What a terrible storm we had one night on the E-RI-E Canal;
We were loaded down with barley, we were all of us full of rye,
And the Captain he looked down on me with a doggone wicked eye.

  O the E-RI-E's a-risin' and the whiskey's gettin' low,
  And I hardly think we'll get a drink,
  Till we get to Buffalo-o-o,
  Till we get to Buffalo.

2 Three days out from Albany a pirate we did spy,
The black flag with the skull and bones was wavin' up on high.
We signaled to the driver to h'iste the flag of truce,
And we found it was the Mary Jane just out of Syracuse. *(Chorus)*

3 The cook, she was a kind old soul, she had a ragged dress,
And we hoisted her upon a pole as a sig-a-nal of distress.
The wind began to whistle and the waves began to roll,
And we had to reef our royals on the rag-i-ing 'Canol'. *(Chorus)*

4 When we got to Syracuse, the offmule he was dead,
The nigh mule got blind staggers, and we cracked him on the head,
The girls are in the Police Gazette, the crew are all in jail,
I'm the only livin' sea-cook's son that's left to tell the tale. *(Chorus)*

The Erie Canal linked the Hudson with the Great Lakes and opened up the Midwest for commerce and settlement. The brawling, hard-drinking Erie canal boatmen composed hundreds of verses, humorously comparing the dangers of the 'raging canal' to the life of the deep-water sailor.

13. WEARY OF THE RAILWAY

Guitarists may capo up one fret and play the chords in brackets.

1 O – in eighteen hundred and forty-one
   My corduroy breeches I put on,
   My corduroy breeches I put on

   To work upon the railway, the railway,
   I'm weary of the railway,
   O poor Paddy works on the railway.

2 O – in eighteen hundred and forty-two
   I did not know what I should do. *(Chorus)*

3 O – in eighteen hundred and forty-three
   I sailed away across the sea. *(Chorus)*

4 O – in eighteen hundred and forty-four
   I landed on Columbia's shore. *(Chorus)*

5 O – in eighteen hundred and forty-five
   When Daniel O'Connel, he was alive. *(Chorus)*

6 O – in eighteen hundred and forty-six
   I changed my trade from carrying bricks. *(Chorus)*

7 O – in eighteen hundred and forty-seven
   Poor Paddy was thinking of going to Heaven. *(Chorus)*

The Irish navvy dug the Erie Canal, and built the railroads in the north of England and the north-eastern United States. Everywhere he swung his pick he sang this Anglo-Irish work song. Versions have been recovered from Manchester, from the clipper-ships, and west as far as San Francisco.

14. THE LITTLE BROWN BULL

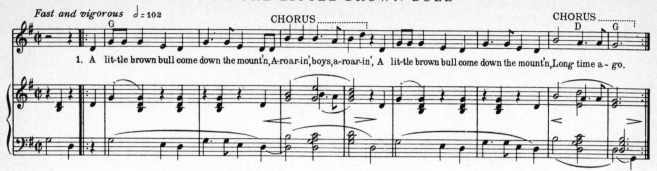

1. A little brown bull come down the mount'n, A-roarin', boys, a-roarin', A little brown bull come down the mount'n, Long time a-go.

1 A little brown bull come down the mount'n,
   A-roarin', boys, a-roarin',
   A little brown bull come down the mount'n
   Long time ago.

2 The little brown bull come down all pizen, *etc.*
   His head in the air, 'n his tail a-risin', *etc.*

3 The little brown bull he made one sally, *etc.*
   An' nine red heifers he found in the valley, *etc.*

4 The little brown bull come down the mount'n, *etc.*
   An' nine bull calves he made that mornin', *etc.*

5 The little brown bull went back to the mount'n, *etc.*
   The nine bull calves became nine oxen, *etc.*

6 The nine red oxen went a-lumberin', *etc.*
   The nine red oxen went a-lumberin', *etc.*

7 They worked themselves all lean and lank, *etc.*
   A-haulin' logs to the river bank, *etc.*

8 When they got old and very much thinner, *etc.*
   They was boiled up for sailors' dinner, *etc.*

Another literature of ballads and shanties arose in the days of sail on the Great Lakes. The narrow, wind-swept lakes have always been dangerous for shipping, and in the days of sail it took a crew of good shanty singers to handle the Great Lakes bark, deep laden with lumber, coal, or iron-ore. All the familiar shanties were sung, and the lake shantyman also made songs of his own, like this epic of *The Little Brown Bull*, known in other forms to deep-water sailors and to midwestern ploughmen.

15. KATY CRUEL

1. When first I came to town They called me the roving jewel, Now they've changed their tune, They call me Katy Cruel. O diddle-olly aye, O a little ly-o-day. day.

1 When first I came to town
   They called me the roving jewel,
   Now they've changed their tune,
   They call me Katy Crúel.
   O diddle-olly-aye,
   O a little ly-o-day.

2 O that I was where I would be
   Then would I be where I am not,
   Here I am where I must be,
   Go where I would I cannot.
   (Chorus)

3 I know who I love,
   And I know who does love me,
   I know where I'll go
   And I know who'll go with me.
   (Chorus)

4 Through the woods I'll go
   And through the boggy mire,
   Straightway on the road
   Till I come to my heart's desire.
   (Chorus then repeat stanza two.)

Katy Cruel is said to have been a camp follower of the American Revolutionary Army. Her song, delivered at a rapid, tongue-twisting pace, flames with intense and bitter passion.

16. THE FOGGY DEW

1. When I was a bachelor, I lived all alone,
   And I worked at the weaver's trade,
   And the only, only thing that I did that was wrong,
   Was to woo a fair young maid.
   I wooed her in the summertime,
   And part of the winter, too,
   And all night long I held her in my arms
   Just to keep her from the foggy, foggy dew.

2. One night she came to my bedside
   When I was fast asleep,
   She threw her arms around my neck
   And bitterly did weep.
   She wept, she cried, she damn near died,
   Poor me what could I do?
   So all night long I held her in my arms
   Just to keep her from the foggy, foggy dew.

3. Again, I am a bachelor and live with my son,
   We work at the weaver's trade.
   And every time I look into his eyes,
   He reminds me of that fair young maid.
   He reminds me of the summertime,
   And part of the winter, too,
   And of the many, many times I held her in my arms
   Just to keep her from the foggy, foggy dew.

The Foggy Dew still current among country singers in southern England tells a much franker story than this American version, which Carl Sandburg discovered and Burl Ives popularized.

II

Southern Mountain Songs

THE APPALACHIAN mountains rise in a dense green tangle along the western borders of Virginia and North Carolina. They occupy the eastern ends of Kentucky and Tennessee, shape the northern borderland of Georgia, and tail off into the hill country of northern Alabama and Mississippi. For some time this formidable, heavily wooded rampart confined the western extension of settlement. Then, in the years before the American Revolution, Daniel Boone charted the trails that led through the Cumberland Gap and into the broad and fertile lands of Kentucky. A tide of settlers poured after him. They were people of English descent who could not find land or place in the aristocratic, slave-holding society of lowland Virginia and North Carolina. They were Germans and Scots-Irish, spilling out of an already crowded Pennsylvania, moving down the long, sweet valley of the Shenandoah and, finally, turning west into Tennessee and Kentucky.

Adventurers, criminals, and frontier hunters travelled among the pioneers, but the majority were farmers looking for good land, where King George's tax gatherers could not find them nor the established Churches interfere with their religious inclinations. The majority were Presbyterians, Baptists, or Methodists. They believed in sin and individual salvation and that God was on their side. They carried a Bible in one hand and a hunting rifle in the other, and in the space of a generation they had completely defeated the Cherokee Indians and their allies, the best-organized and the best-led Indian tribes the pioneers would encounter until they fought the western Sioux.

This mountain society, formed in the midst of bloody Indian wars and wrapped in mountain isolation, held to the tradition of the blood feud which the Scots settlers may have brought with them. A strain of frontier violence still runs strongly in the blood of its people. The last of the mountain feuds did not die down until the 1930s, and when I visited Eastern Kentucky in 1937 I was told that square dancing had died out in many communities because there had been so many killings by jealous mountain men with bellies full of moonshine whiskey.

The tide of western settlement soon left this mountain wilderness behind. Until this century only a few roads and railroads had penetrated its remote hollows, and life continued to develop in the patterns laid down in the eighteenth century. Feuding and moonshining were only one aspect of this culture; far more important and characteristic were an antique gentleness of manner, a genuine native refinement, and a rich regional culture.

The mountaineer's manners, tempered by rural shyness and country cordiality, indicate clearly that he thinks he is as good a man as you are, if not a bit better. Money and property matter less to him than the freedom and independence of the life he enjoys among his laurel-covered hills. His corn fields may run almost straight up and down, so 'you have to tie a rope around yer middle to keep from fallin' out of um', but he knows how to 'make out anyhow', supplementing a meagre crop with what he can earn with his axe and his gun.

His vocabulary is a rich weave of old English and frontier lingo. He speaks of a *feisty* (impertinent, out of Chaucer) man, and a *sevigrous* (shrewish, out of the frontier) woman, and of going to an *infare* (which means wedding or just party in the mountains, but meant a pre-nuptial party for the bridegroom in old England). He says, 'We-uns didn't hyear no-give out about it', meaning 'we hadn't heard anything about it'. He rejoices in the doubled and re-doubled negative – 'I never did see no man of no kind do no washing.' *Ary* and *nary* stand for the ancient *e'er a* and *ne'er a*. But, although he retains many archaisms of speech, he often takes pleasure in treating the language with untrammelled pioneer freedom, speaking of 'the green shadder gum tree', 'lick-spittin' on down the road', and in laying the accent where he pleases, 'can't come to no agree*ment*, we're too hos*tile*.'

In his rich folklore the pattern is the same. Little Jack, the hero of the English *märchen*, turns up in overalls in the Smoky Mountains. Scots witches inhabit the Ozarks. At a mountain singing one hears ballads that pre-date Shakespeare, followed by songs about wrecks on the highway. The mood of most of the older songs is quietly melancholy, suitable to the spare, hard, and lonely life in mountain cabins, and shot through with the Calvinist conviction that love and pleasure are wicked. This nostalgic and tragic school of songs is counterbalanced by the ramping, tearing rhythms of the ditties sung by the dancing, drinking, hell-raising crowd of young men. Strictly religious families totally ban both these types of songs as sinful and devilish, and confine themselves to singing spirituals, which are often set to the same tunes as the 'love songs'.

This folk culture is not peculiar to the mountains; it merely reached its peak of development there. All the southern backwoods were settled by the same group of people in about the same period, bearing a common culture and faced with common problems. Thus the same songs, the same patterns of preference, and the same lore may be found, though in varying degrees of intensity, among the 'poor whites' throughout the South as far west as Texas and Oklahoma.

17. PRETTY SARO

1 Way down in the lone valley, in some lonesome place,
  I wish no better pastime than to be with my sweet,
  But she says she won't have me, so that I understand
  She wants some freeholder, where I have no land.

2 I cannot maintain her with silver and gold,
  Nor buy her all the fine things that a big house can hold.
  So farewell, pretty Saro, I bid thee adieu,
  I'm going to ramble this whole world all through.

3 If I were a merchant and could write some fine hand,
  I would write my love a letter that she might understand.
  I would send it by the river where the water do flow,
  And I'll think of pretty Saro wherever I go.

4 I wish I were a dove and had wings and could fly,
  This night to my love's window I would draw nigh.
  And in her lily-white arms all night I would lay,
  And watch them little windows to the dawning of the day.

This song refers, fleetingly, to the motive which forced many settlers into the wild and rugged mountain country. All available good land in the lowland South had been taken up by the time of the American Revolution, and the 'poor white' who wished to better himself had to move on west. This love-sick frontiersman feels 'lonesome'; he is not sure that he is wanted or has roots anywhere. This 'lonesome' feeling increasingly pervaded Southern songs, giving rise, ultimately, to the *lonesome blues* of the Negro.

18. THE LAZY MAN

1. I'll sing you a song that's not very long, A-bout a la-zy farm-er would-n't hoe his corn, The rea-son why I can-not tell, For that young man was al-ways well, For that young man was al-ways well.

1 I'll sing you a song that's not very long,
  About a lazy farmer wouldn't hoe his corn,
  The reason why I cannot tell,
  For that young man was always well. *(twice)*

2 He went to his field and he peeped in,
  The weeds and grass were up to his chin,
  The bushes and the grass grew so high,
  Enough for to make this young man sigh. *(twice)*

3 Now that winter I am told,
  He went a-courtin' very bold,
  And when his courtin' had begun,
  'Tell me, young man, did you make any corn?' *(twice)*

4 He answered her in this reply,
  'No, kind miss, I've laid it by,
  It wasn't worth while to strive in vain,
  For I know I won't make one grain.' *(twice)*

5 'Here you come, wantin' me to wed.
  And cannot make your own cornbread,
  Single I am and single I'll remain,
  For a lazy man I won't maintain. *(twice)*

6 'Go on down to that pretty little widder,
  And I hope, by heck, that you don't git her . . .
  She gave him the mitten sure's you're born,
  All because he wouldn't hoe corn. *(twice)*

No poem so accurately recreates the atmosphere of frontier life as does this simple little rural satire. One can imagine it sung in dialogue form at pioneer gatherings, causing laughter, yet driving home its lesson well, for corn was the staple food of the white settlers, as it had been among the Indians.

19. WENT UP ON THE MOUNTAIN

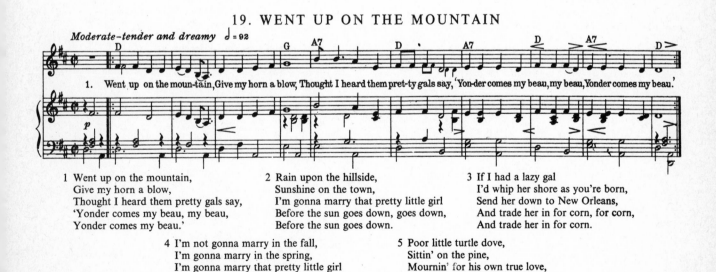

1. Went up on the moun-tain, Give my horn a blow, Thought I heard them pret-ty gals say, 'Yon-der comes my beau, my beau, Yonder comes my beau.'

1 Went up on the mountain,
  Give my horn a blow,
  Thought I heard them pretty gals say,
  'Yonder comes my beau, my beau,
  Yonder comes my beau.'

2 Rain upon the hillside,
  Sunshine on the town,
  I'm gonna marry that pretty little girl
  Before the sun goes down, goes down,
  Before the sun goes down.

3 If I had a lazy gal
  I'd whip her shore as you're born,
  Send her down to New Orleans,
  And trade her in for corn, for corn,
  And trade her in for corn.

4 I'm not gonna marry in the fall,
  I'm gonna marry in the spring,
  I'm gonna marry that pretty little girl
  Who wears the golden ring, ring,
  Who wears the golden ring.

5 Poor little turtle dove,
  Sittin' on the pine,
  Mournin' for his own true love,
  Just as I mourn for mine, for mine,
  Just as I mourn for mine.

This Smoky Mountain love song captures the wild charm of those green, misty hills, where patterns of American pioneer life have endured into our own time. Like so many American folk lyrics, it is a catch-all for verses from many sources, some American, some, like the turtle dove stanza, of British origin.

20. COME ALL YOU VIRGINIA GIRLS

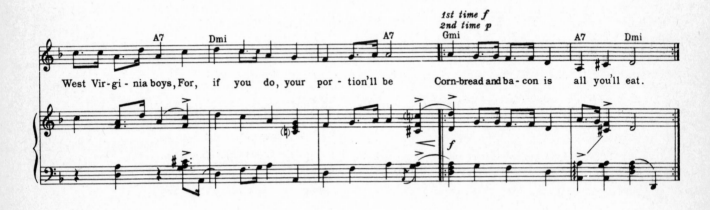

1 Come all you Virginia girls and listen to my noise,
  Don't go with those West Virginia boys,
  For, if you do, your portion'll be
  Cornbread and bacon is all you'll eat,
  Cornbread and bacon is all you'll eat.

2 When they come a-courtin' they bring along a chair,
  First thing they say, 'Has your daddy killed a deer?'
  Next thing they say, when they sit down,
  'Madam, your Johnny-Cake's too damn brown.' *(twice)*

3 When they come a-courtin', I'll tell you what they wear,
  An old leather coat all picked and bare,
  An old straw hat more brim than crown,
  And a pair of dirty socks they've worn the winter round. *(twice)*

4 They'll take you out on some lonesome hill,
  There they'll leave you all against your will,
  They'll starve you in the valley and they'll leave you in the plain,
  That's the way with the West Virgin-i-ans. *(twice)*

5 Now brandy's brandy anyway you mix it,
  A Virginian's a Virginian any way you fix him,
  When other good folks have gone to bed,
  The devil gets to working in the West Virginian's head. *(twice)*

The people of the settled lowlands of Virginia composed this satirical song, warning their girls of the life they would face if they married a man from the wild mountain country of West Virginia. As the frontier moved west, the song travelled west as well; the names of the states were changed, but the essence of the warning remained the same.

21. GROUND-HOG

1 Whet up yer knife and whistle up yer dogs, *(twice)*
Away to the hills to catch ground-hogs.
     Ground-Hog!

2 They picked up their guns and went to the braish, *(twice)*
By damn, Bill, here's a hog-sign fraish. *(Refrain)*

3 Hunker down, Sam, and in there peep, *(twice)*
For I think I see him sound asleep. *(Refrain)*

4 Run here, Johnny, with a great long pole. *(twice)*
And roust this ground-hog outer his hole. *(Refrain)*

5 Work, boys, work, as hard as you can tear, *(twice)*
This meat'll do to eat and the hide'll do to wear. *(Refrain)*

6 I heard him give a whistle and a wail, *(twice)*
And I wound my stick around his tail. *(Refrain)*

7 Scrape him down to his head and feet, *(twice)*
Lordy, boys, there's a fine pile o' meat. *(Refrain)*

8 They put him in the pot and all began to smile, *(twice)*
They et that ground hog 'fore he struck a bile. *(Refrain)*

9 The children screamed and the children cried, *(twice)*
They love ground-hog cooked and fried. *(Refrain)*

10 Up stepped Sal with a snigger and a grin, *(twice)*
Groundhog grease all over her chin. *(Refrain)*

11 Run here, Mama, run here, quick, *(twice)*
I think that ground-hog's makin' me sick. *(Refrain)*

12 Run here, Mama, make Bill quit, *(twice)*
He's et all the ground-hog an' I ain't had a bit. *(Refrain)*

13 Ol' Aunt Sal come a-skippin' through the hall, *(twice)*
Got enough ground-hog to feed um all.

    GROUND-HOG!

Spring, according to many backwoods weather prophets, begins the first day that the ground-hog sticks his head out of his burrow and can see his own shadow. Then you can safely spade your garden and plant the first seeds.

In the Kentucky mountains they hunt the ground-hog (wood-chuck), roast him like a possum and eat him with gusto, as this humorous epic tells. One of the best banjo tunes, this song is the discovery of Josiah Combs.

22. OLD BLUE

1 I had an ol' dog, boys, and I called him Blue,
Listen lemme tell you what Blue could do.
CHORUS 1: Come on, Blue, you good dog, you.
Yes, come on, Blue, you good dog, you.

2 I took my axe, boys, and I blowed my horn,
Goin' a-huntin' just as shore's you're born. *(Chorus 1)*

3 Old Blue treed and I went to see,
Had him a possum up a white-oak tree. *(Chorus 1)*

4 He growled at me, I looked at him,
I shook him out, Blue took him in. *(Chorus 1)*

5 Baked that possum good and brown,
Laid them sweet 'taters round and round.
CHORUS 2: *Says, come on, Blue, you can have some, too.*
Yes, come on, Blue, you can have some, too.

6 The doctor come, an' he come on the run,
He says, 'Old Blue, your huntin' is done.' *(Chorus 1)*

7 Old Blue died, an' he died so hard,
He dug up the ground all over the yard.
CHORUS 3 *Go on, Blue, you good dog, you,*
Yes, go on, Blue, you good dog, you.

8 When I get to heaven, I know what I'll do,
Grab my horn and blow for old Blue.
CHORUS 4: *Sayin' 'Come here Blue, I've got here, too.' (twice)*

9 And when I hear my old Blue dog bark,
I'll know he's treed a 'possum in Noah's Ark. *(Chorus 4)*

This folk elegy to the Southern hound dog is the product of the old south west (Mississippi, Arkansas, and Texas) where a good hunting dog meant meat on the table in bad years and good. Sung in a straight, hard, flat back-woods voice, there is not a hint of comedy or sentimentality in this simple ballad. The singer simply regards Old Blue as a member of his family. John A. Lomax recorded this version in Fort Spunky, Texas, in 1942.

23. THE FARMER'S CURST WIFE

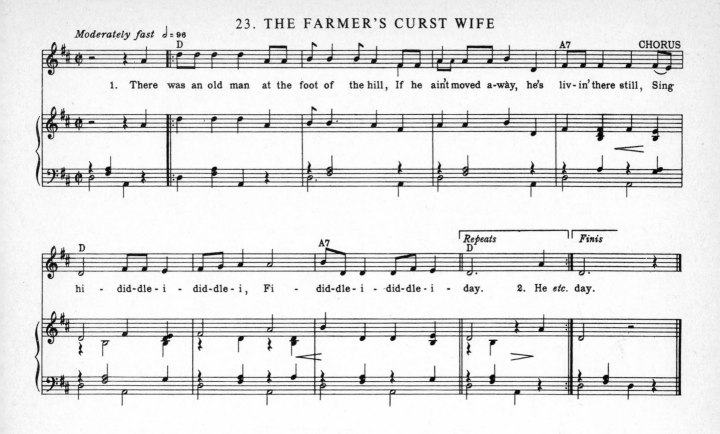

1 There was an old man at the foot of the hill,
  If he ain't moved away, he's livin' there still,
    Sing hi-diddle-i-diddle-i,
    Fi-diddle-i-diddle-i-day.

2 He hitched up his horse and he went out to plough,
  But how to get around he didn't know how. *(Chorus)*

3 The devil come to his house one day,
  Says, 'One of your family I'm a-gonna take away.' *(Chorus)*

4 'Take her, take her with all of my heart,
  And I hope, by gollies, you never part.' *(Chorus)*

5 The devil put her up on his back,
  And off to Hell he went, clickity-clack. *(Chorus)*

6 When he got her down to the gates of hell,
  He says, 'Punch up the fire, we'll scorch her well.' *(Chorus)*

7 In come a little devil, a-draggin' a chain,
  She upped with a hatchet and split out his brain. *(Chorus)*

8 Nine little devils went a-climbin' the wall,
  Says, 'Take her back, daddy, she's a-murderin' us all.' *(Chorus)*

9 The old man was a-peepin' out of a crack,
  And saw the old Devil come draggin' her back. *(Chorus)*

10 She found the old man sick in his bed,
   She upped with a butter stick and paddled his head. *(Chorus)*

11 The old woman went whistlin' over the hill,
   'The devil won't have me, I wonder who will.' *(Chorus)*

21 There's one advantage women have over men,
   They can go to hell and come back again. *(Chorus)*

A great many European medieval ballads have been found in a livelier state of preservation in backwoods America than in Europe. These ballads linked the settlers with their homeland; they provided music and poetry for isolated frontier cabins; they were the songs the pioneer woman sang to amuse her children and help pass away the lonely hours of her life. Their importance in American culture is shown by the fact that they have been found not only in the Southern Appalachians, but in the North, the Middle West, and the West, as well. *Barbara Allen* has always been America's most popular romantic folk ballad, and this story of the scolding wife is the all-out favourite on the comic side. A Virginia mountain version.

24. PRETTY POLLY

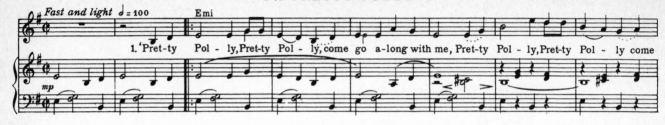

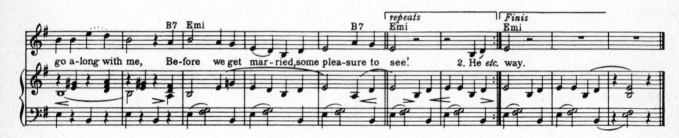

1 'Pretty Polly, Pretty Polly, come go along with me, *(twice)*
Before we get married, some pleasure to see.'

2 He led her over hills and valleys so deep, *(twice)*
Till at last Pretty Polly began for to weep.

3 'O Willy, O Willy, I'm feared of your way, *(twice)*
I fear you are leading your poor Polly astray.'

4 They rode on a piece further and what did she spy, *(twice)*
But a new-made grave and a spade lying by.

5 'Pretty Polly, Pretty Polly, you're thinkin' just right, *(twice)*
I dug on your grave the best part of the night.'

6 She fell down on her knees and she suffered no fear, *(twice)*
'How can you kill a poor girl that loves you so dear?'

7 He stabbed her to the heart, which caused the blood to flow, *(twice)*
And down in the grave her pale body he throwed.

8 He covered her over and started for home, *(twice)*
Leavin' only the small birds to lament and to moan.

9 A debt to the Devil poor Willy must pay, *(twice)*
For killin' Pretty Polly and runnin' away.

In the nineteenth century, the theme of the innocent girl, betrayed and murdered by her sweetheart, was the favourite theme for rural ballad makers in the U.S. *Pretty Polly* derives from the English *Gosport Tragedy*, first published about 1750 and running to thirty odd stanzas. Mountain banjo pickers have condensed and simplified the Grub Street original, thus creating a powerful and tragic ballad, and showing clearly that songs may often be improved in oral transmission. Another typical banjo-accompanied song.

25. I LOVE MY LOVE

1. All my friends fell out with me Be-cause I kept my love's com-pa-ny, But let them say or do what they will, I love my love with a free good will.

1 All my friends fell out with me
  Because I kept my love's company,
  But let them say or do what they will,
  I love my love with a free good will.

2 Over the mountain I must go
  Because my fortune is so low;
  With an aching heart and a troubled mind
  For leaving my true love behind.

3 The Powers above look down and see
  The parting of true love and me,
  'Tis as hard to part the moon and sky
  As it is to part true love and I.

4 When I have gold she has her part,
  And when I have none she has my heart;
  And she gained it, too, with a free good will,
  And upon my honor I love her still.

5 The winter's past and summer's come,
  The trees are budding one by one,
  And when my true love chooses to stay,
  I'll stay with her till the break of day.

British lyric song styles flowered in the mountains, giving rise to many new songs, of which this may be one. Here, however, is a mountain love song which has kept a trace of the frankness so characteristic of the Southern English and Scots songs. It was found in the North Carolina mountains by Cecil Sharp.

26. MY GOOD OLD MAN

1 Where have you been, my good old man?
  O where have you been, my honey-lovey dove?
  Where have you been, my good old man?
      You're the best old man in the world.
  SPOKEN: Been to the store.

2 What did you git me, my good old man? *etc.* *(Chorus)*
  SPOKEN: Bought ye a dress.

3 How much did it cost you, my good old man? *etc.* *(Chorus)*
  SPOKEN: 'Bout fifty cents.

4 Ain't you 'fraid that'll break you, my good old man? *etc.* *(Chorus)*
  SPOKEN: Don't keer if it do.

5 What ye want for yer supper, my good old man? *etc.* *(Chorus)*
  SPOKEN: A dozen bushels of eggs.

6 Ain't ye 'fraid they'll choke ye, my good old man? *etc.* *(Chorus)*
  SPOKEN: Don't keer if they do.

7 Whur ye want to be buried at, my good old man? *etc.* *(Chorus)*
  SPOKEN: In the corner by the chimney place.

8 Ain't ye 'fraid of snuffin' ashes, my good old man? *etc.* *(Chorus)*
  SPOKEN: Don't keer if I do,
          So long as I'm near you, Sal.

A comic courting song that travelled from the Welsh countryside and took root again in the Kentucky Mountains, where we found it in a coal-mining camp in the summer of 1937.

27. WILL YOU WEAR RED?

Rather fast, light ♩ = 100

1. O will you wear red, O my dear, O my dear? Will you wear red, Jen-nie Jen-kins? won't wear red, it's the col-our of my head. I'll buy me a twir-ley-whir-ley, sook-ey-look-ey, Sal-ly-Kat-ty, dou-ble-lol-ly, Roll - the-find-me, roll, Jen-nie Jen-kins, roll.

---

1 O will you wear red, O my dear, O my dear?
Will you wear red, Jennie Jenkins?
I won't wear red, it's the colour of my head.
I'll buy me a twirley-whirley, sookey-lookey,
Sally-Katty, double-lolly,
Roll-the-find-me, roll, Jennie Jenkins, roll.

2 O will you wear blue, *etc.*
Will you wear blue, *etc.*
I won't wear blue, for I won't be true, *(Chorus)*

3 O will you wear yaller, *etc.*
Will you wear yaller, *etc.*
I won't wear yaller, I've got the wrong feller, *(Chorus)*

4 O will you wear green, *etc.*
Will you wear green, *etc.*
I won't wear green, for I'm 'shamed to be seen, *(Chorus)*

5 O will you wear brown, *etc.*
Will you wear brown, *etc.*
I won't wear brown and live out of town, *(Chorus)*

6 O will you wear purple, *etc.*
Will you wear purple, *etc.*
I won't wear purple it's the colour of a turkle, *(Chorus)*

7 O what will you wear, o my dear, o my dear?
What will you wear, Jennie Jenkins?
Now what do you care if I just go bare! *(Chorus)*

This answer-back song brought together many a shy courting couple at frontier sociables in New England and the Southern mountains. The boy named the colours, and it was up to the girl to find a rhyming line, the sillier the better. In this atmosphere of rural spoofery, the colour rhymes gradually lost the ritual significance that they had in earlier songs like *Miss Jennia Jones*. So it was in the version which we found in the Blue Ridge Mountains of Virginia. But in the Ozarks, Vance Randolph found the rhyme,

Blue is true,
Yeller's jealous,
Green's forsaken,
Red is brazen,
White is love
And black is death.

47

28. LOLLY TOODUM

Moderately fast ♩=120

1. As I went out one morn-in' to breathe the pleasant air, Lol-ly-too-dum, too-dum, lol-ly-too-dum-day. As I went out one morn-in' to breathe the pleasant air, I o-ver heard a moth-er a-scold-in' her daugh-ter fair, Lol-ly-too-dum, too-dum, lol-ly-too-dum-day. 2. 'You *etc.* day.

1 As I went out one mornin' to breathe the pleasant air,
  Lolly-too-dum, too-dum, lolly-too-dum-day.
As I went out one mornin' to breathe the pleasant air,
I overheard a mother a-scoldin' her daughter fair,
  Lolly-too-dum, too-dum, lolly-too-dum-day.

2 'You better go wash them dishes and hush that flatterin' tongue, *etc.*
  You know that you want to get married and that you air too young.' *etc.*

3 'O pity my condition just as you would your own, *etc.*
  For fourteen long years I have lived all alone.' *etc.*

4 'Now if I was to be willin' where would you get your man?' *etc.*
  'O lawsy massy, mammy, I'd marry handsome Sam.' *etc.*

5 'There's lawyers and doctors and boys from the plow.' *etc.*
  'O lawsy massy, mammy, the fit comes on me now.' *etc.*

6 'Now my daughter's married and well for to do, *etc.*
  Come gather round, young fellers, I'm on the market, too.' *etc.*

Women were scarce in the Southern colonies and girls married young. The first great American jurist, Chief Justice Marshall, fell in love with a thirteen-year-old girl and married her at sixteen. Some girls married at thirteen, many by fifteen, and an unmarried woman of twenty-five was considered a hopeless and confirmed old maid. These attitudes still persist to some extent in remote sections of the Southern Appalachians. A gnarled mountain farmer named Abner Boggs sang this satirical country dialogue for me in Harlan County, his voice so high and lonesome you could hear him literally a mile away.

29. OLD MAN'S COURTSHIP

First 5 bars Moderate, free, then quick and rhythmical

1 Old man come courtin' me one day,
    But I won't have him,
  He come down the lane,
  Just a-leanin' on his cane,
  And his durned old beard a-waggin'.

2 My mama told me to ask him in,
    But I wouldn't have him,
  Well, I asked him in
  And he bit me on the chin,
  With his durned old beard a-waggin'.

3 My mama told me to hand him a chair,
    But I won't have him,
  I handed him a chair,
  And he ran like a deer,
  With his durned old beard a-waggin'.

4 My mama told me to light him to bed,
    But I wouldn't have him,
  I lit him to bed,
  And he slept like he's dead,
  With his durned old beard a-waggin'.

5 My mama told me to kiss him goodbye,
    My, I won't have him,
  I kissed him goodbye,
  And I thought I'd die,
  With his durned old beard a-waggin'.

6 Now I'm goin' to get me a nice young man,
    Yes, I'm a-gonna have him,
  A nice young man
  Who'll kiss me all he can,
  And no durned beard a-waggin'.

The Kentucky mountain woman who gave me this song explained that on occasion it had been sung by a young girl to shame her parents who were attempting to marry her off to a rich old man. The song is widespread in Great Britain.

30. EAST VIRGINIA

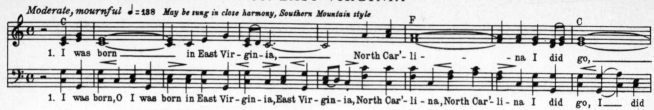

1 I was born in East Virginia,
   North Car'lina I did go,
   There I courted a pretty young woman,
   And her age I did not know.

2 Her hair was of some brightsome colour,
   Her cheeks were of a rosy red,
   On her breast she wore white lilies,
   Many a tear for her I've shed.

3 In my heart you are my darlin',
   At my door you're welcome in,
   At my gate, I'll always meet you,
   If your love I could only win.

4 When I'm asleep I'm dreaming of you,
   When I'm awake I see no rest,
   Moments seem to me like hours,
   With achin' pains all acrost my breast.

5 I'd rather be in some dark holler,
   Where the sun refuse to shine,
   Than to see you another man's darlin',
   And to know you'll never be mine.

6 When I am dead and in my coffin,
   With my pale face towards the sun,
   You can come and see me darlin',
   See the deed that you have done.

Western Virginia, the wild, mountainous region across the Appalachians, was settled by poor white Calvinists. It never felt itself a part of the slave-owning South, and in 1860 it separated from 'Eastern Virginia', set up its own State Government and allied itself with the Union. This song, dating from the period, comes from the mountainous borders of East Virginia. Like so many mountain love songs, it is laden with a sense of despair and frustration and a melancholy brooding about death. These frontier folk were weighed down with a Calvinist feeling of the shamefulness of the flesh. The rather nonsensical line

On her breast she wore white lilies

may once have been

And her breasts were white as lilies

31. SINGLE GIRL

Fast and flowing ♩ = 116

lightly

1. Sin-gle girl,____ sin-gle girl,____ She's go-in' dressed so fine;____

Mar-ried girl,____ mar-ried girl,____ She wears just a - ny

kind, Oh ____ she wears just a - ny kind.____

1 Single girl, single girl,
  She's goin' dressed so fine;
  Married girl, married girl,
  She wears just any kind,
  Oh – she wears just any kind.

2 Single girl, single girl,
  Goes to the store and buys;
  Married girl, married girl,
  She rocks the cradle and cries.
  Oh – she rocks the cradle and cries.

3 Single girl, single girl,
  Goin' where she please;
  Married girl, married girl,
  Has a baby on her knees,
  Oh – baby on her knees.

The life of the mountain woman was one of complete subservience to her menfolk; she milked the cows, kept the garden, fetched water from a distant spring, cooked and cleaned in a primitive log cabin and waited on her men at table, never sitting down to eat until all the males had finished their meal. The normal family consisted of ten to twenty children and the girls, who often married at twelve or thirteen, often looked like old women at thirty. One old crone, advising a young girl about marriage, simply said, 'Don't never do hit!'

51

32. GOOBER PEAS

1 Sittin' by the road side on a summer day,
  Chattin' with my mess-mates, passin' time away,
  Lyin' in the shadow underneath the trees,
  Goodness, how delicious, eatin' goober peas.
      Peas, peas, peas, peas, eatin' goober peas,
      Goodness, how delicious, eatin' goober peas.

2 When a horseman passes, the soldiers have a rule,
  To cry out at their loudest, 'Mister, here's your mule,'
  But another pleasure, enchantinger than these,
  Is wearing out your grinders, eating goober peas. *(Chorus)*

3 Just before the battle the Gen'ral hears a row,
  He says, 'The Yanks are coming, I hear their rifles now.'
  He turns around in wonder, and what do you think he sees?
  The Georgia Militia, eating goober peas. *(Chorus)*

4 I think my song has lasted almost long enough,
  The subject's interesting, but the rhymes are mighty rough,
  I wish this war was over, when free from rags and fleas,
  We'd kiss our wives and sweethearts, and gobble goober peas. *(Chorus)*

The Civil War, the War Between the States, was a singing war. Among the scores of marching songs, sung by soldiers, blue and grey, was this rebel satire on the rationing of chickpeas to the starving Southern troops.

33. WAKE UP, DARLIN' COREY

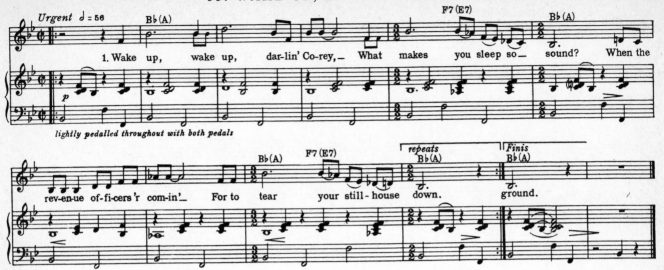

lightly pedalled throughout with both pedals

1. Wake up, wake up, dar-lin' Co-rey,— What makes you sleep so— sound? When the rev-en-ue of-fi-cers 'r com-in'— For to tear your still-house down. ground.

1 Wake up, wake up, darlin' Corey,
What makes you sleep so sound?
When the revenue officers are comin'
For to tear your still-house down.

2 The first time I saw darlin' Corey,
She had a wine glass in her hand,
Drinkin' that cold pizen liquor
With a lowdown, sorry man.

3 The next time I saw darlin' Corey
She was standin' in her door,
With her shoes and stockin's in her hand
And her feet all over the floor.

4 The last time I saw darlin' Corey
She was standin' on the banks of the sea,
A pistol strapped round her body
And her banjo on her knee.

5 Go 'way from me, darlin' Corey,
Quit hangin' round my bed,
Pretty womens' run me distracted,
Corn liquor's killed me stone dead.

6 Don't you hear them bluebirds singin',
Don't you hear that lonesome sound,
They're preachin' darlin' Corey's funeral
In the lonesome graveyard ground.

The most profitable way for a mountain farmer to dispose of his small corn (Indian Maize) crop is to distil it into whiskey and sell it as untaxed spirits (mountain moonshine). His battle with the revenuer (customs official) has gone on since the time of George Washington, and there are still lonesome valleys in the Kentucky mountains where revenuers are unwanted intruders. This banjo song must be sung with long, sustained, lonesome notes and a fast moving accompaniment.

34. DARLIN'

1 Darlin', you can't love one,
   Darlin', you can't love one,
   You can't love one and have any fun,
   Darlin', you can't love one.

2 Darlin', you can't love two, *(twice)*
   You can't love two and to me be true,
   Darlin' you can't love two.

Stanzas three to ten may be rhymed out as follows.
. . . and get along with me.
. . . and come knocking at my door.
. . . and get honey from my hive.
. . . and keep me in this fix.
. . . and expect to go to Heaven.
. . . and keep this business straight.
. . . and see me all the time.
. . . and be welcome here again.

Some hillbilly, who came to town and discovered the limitations of his ancestral Calvinism, began this rhyme, and it has kept on rolling by itself from coast to coast, to become the national chant of a rebellious American libido.

III

Lullabies and Reels

FOLK lullabies occur rarely in British collections, and even less frequently in the United States. Only the old-fashioned Negro 'mammies' had any considerable number of songs which, words and music, were designed to lull children to sleep. (See No. 37 for the best and most characteristic of these.) Most of the women I questioned told me they rocked their children to sleep with anything they were in the mood for themselves – with ballads, love songs or old time hymns. Slow, dreamy, sad songs were normally chosen.

By contrast, Americans sang scores of baby-bouncing songs, jig-jog ditties, tickling rhymes, toe-counting formulas, comical jingles, and funny old ballads to amuse children. (See Nos. 40, 41.) Most of these have no tunes to speak of.

> Me and my wife and a stump-tailed dog
> Crossed Cane River on a hickory log,
> The log did break and she fell in,
> Lost my wife and a bottle of gin.

The songs of the children themselves would require a special volume in many languages. For one thing, a great number of the best and oldest British game-songs are still kept alive in villages and big towns. One hears garbled fragments of the old shepherds' system of counting,

> Onery, uery, ickery see,
> Huckabone, crackabone, tillibonee,
> Ramp pang, muski dan,
> Striddleum, straddleum, twenty-one.

alongside of new folk rhymes right off the city streets,

(A TAUNT)   Liar, liar, your pants are on fire,
           Your nose is as long as a telephone wire.

(LIKEWISE)   Roses are red, violets are blue,
           I like pecans, nuts to you . . .

(ROPE-SKIPPING)   My mother, your mother lives across the way,
           Three-sixteen, East Broadway,
           Every night they have a fight, and this is what they say;
           'Lady moon, lady moon, turn around, round, round,
           Lady moon, lady moon, touch the ground, ground, ground.'

But the most original of our children's rhymes and tunes may still be heard accompanying wonderfully graceful dancing among Negroes in the Deep South. (See No. 39.)

To the whites these songs seemed fragments of pure fantasy, catching in their rippling syllables the precise rhythms of the clapping, patting, dancing rhythms they accompanied. Coons, possums, hound dogs, terrapins, snakes, june bugs, and scores of other humble animals of southern woods and fields came to life in these little jingles; but, if one cared to look slightly below their humorous surface, one could see how these characters were masquerading for slave and master, Negro and white. Old Brer Rabbit of song and story, big-eyed, timid, agile, and witty, played the part of the Negro slave, who managed to find pleasures and enjoy his freedom even with the white overseer one jump behind.

Up until the 1880s the African Bamboula, accompanied by African drums, was danced out at Mardi Gras on Congo Square in New Orleans; but the majority of slave dances at southern corn-huskings, quilting bees, syrup-stirrings, and log-rollings were syncopated adaptations of British reels and jigs. (See Nos. 42, 45.) Indeed, such proficient jiggers were the slaves that the vulgar still refer to Negroes as 'jigs'.

One day in 1936 I photographed a Negro woman worker in one of the big Florida vegetable farms doing a crow dance. Arms swinging wide, she stooped and hopped about in rhythm to her song until one could truly imagine a big black bird dancing to an African rhythm. It was just such a dance that Daddy Rice, the originator of the minstrel show, spied on the wharf of Cincinnati. He dragged the astonished Negro roustabout to his dressing room, donned his ragged clothes, blacked his face, and came on to the stage and did an imitation of the long-shoreman's dance, singing the little Negro ditty,

> Turn about and wheel about and do just so,
> And every time I wheel about, I jump Jim Crow.

Both dance and song proved a tremendous hit and inaugurated a hundred years of minstrel show, which kept Negro songs and pseudo-songs constantly ringing in America's ear, although it was almost a hundred years before Negro entertainers managed to break through the race-line (ironically called the Jim Crow line) and begin to play their rightful part in America's entertainment industry. Meanwhile, songs and dances had been so often swapped back and forth across the Jim Crow barrier, that it became hard to distinguish between which were Negro and which were white. Nor is that as important as the fact that white and Negro musicians in the South imitated, emulated, and competed with each other to the great benefit of Southern folk music. Frontiersmen in Tennessee, Arkansas, Missouri, Kansas, and on west called and danced fantastic new forms of the old British reels, their fiddle bows shaking, their heels rocking to Scots-Irish-Negro rhythms.

> I danced with a gal with a hole in her stockin',
> And her heel kep' a-rockin' an' her toe kep' a-knockin',
> I danced with a gal with a hole in her stockin'
> And I danced by the light of the moon.

When no fiddler or banjo player was handy – and fiddles were scarcer than hoopskirts on the frontier – the Celtic (or Negro) talent for making 'chin-music' came into play. A rowdy genre of songs, called reels or fiddle songs, thus came into being.

35. COTTON-EYE JOE

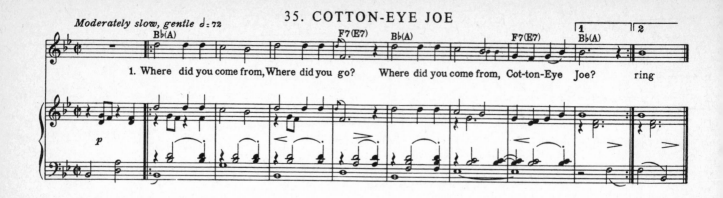

1. Where did you come from, Where did you go? Where did you come from, Cot-ton-Eye Joe? ring

1 Where did you come from,
  Where did you go?
  Where did you come from,
  Cotton-Eye Joe?

2 Come for to see you,
  Come for to sing,
  Come for to show you
  My diamond ring.

In Southern parlance a man is 'cotton-eyed' if his irises are milky-coloured. Cotton-Eye Joe, the obscure hero of a number of Negro dancing tunes and fiddler's airs, here turns up in one of the loveliest of Southern mountain lullabies, found by Margaret Valliant in the hills of Tennessee.

36. THE OLD GREY GOOSE

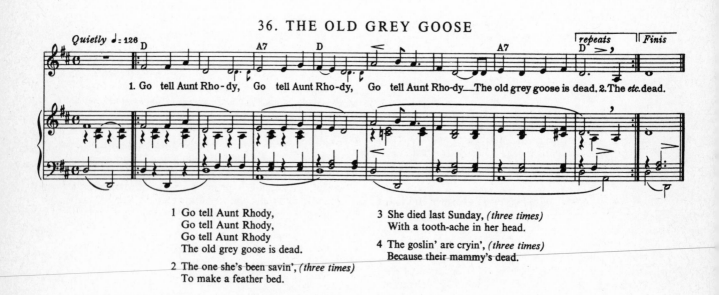

1. Go tell Aunt Rho-dy, Go tell Aunt Rho-dy, Go tell Aunt Rho-dy__ The old grey goose is dead. 2. The etc. dead.

1 Go tell Aunt Rhody,
  Go tell Aunt Rhody,
  Go tell Aunt Rhody
  The old grey goose is dead.

2 The one she's been savin', *(three times)*
  To make a feather bed.

3 She died last Sunday, *(three times)*
  With a tooth-ache in her head.

4 The goslin' are cryin', *(three times)*
  Because their mammy's dead.

Based on a melodic formula, widespread in folk song, especially in children's songs, this tune is, by some, attributed to Jean-Jacques Rousseau, to whom it is said to have come in a dream. This nursery jingle became the universal lullaby of the white pioneers and has been found in every part of America as *Aunt Tabby, Aunt Sarah, Aunt Nancy,* etc.

37. HUSH-YOU-BYE

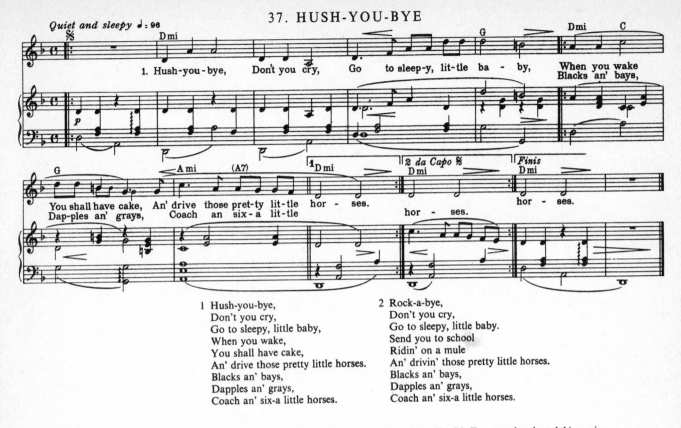

1 Hush-you-bye,
Don't you cry,
Go to sleepy, little baby,
When you wake,
You shall have cake,
An' drive those pretty little horses.
Blacks an' bays,
Dapples an' grays,
Coach an' six-a little horses.

2 Rock-a-bye,
Don't you cry,
Go to sleepy, little baby.
Send you to school
Ridin' on a mule
An' drivin' those pretty little horses.
Blacks an' bays,
Dapples an' grays,
Coach an' six-a little horses.

A Negro 'mammy's' lullaby, known throughout the South to Negro and white mothers alike. My Texan mother shaped this version.

38. HUSH, LITTLE BABY

1 Hush, little baby, don't say a word,
Mama's gonna buy you a mockin' bird.

2 If that mockin' bird don't sing,
Mama's gonna buy you a diamond ring.

3 If that diamond ring turns brass,
Mama's gonna buy you a lookin' glass.

4 If that lookin' glass gets broke,
Mama's gonna buy you a billy-goat.

5 If that billy-goat won't pull,
Mama's gonna buy you a cart and bull.

6 If that cart and bull turn over,
Mama's gonna buy you a dog named Rover.

7 If that dog named Rover don't bark,
Mama's gonna buy you a horse and cart.

8 If that horse and cart fall down,
You'll be the sweetest little girl in town.

This British ditty for soothing and amusing a baby was sung to us by an Alabama Negro woman. In the Ozark hills, where they remember the old belief that a mirror clouds over for a girl who has lost her virtue, they have this verse,

If that lookin' glass don't shine,
Papa's gonna shoot that beau of mine.

59

39. ALL HID

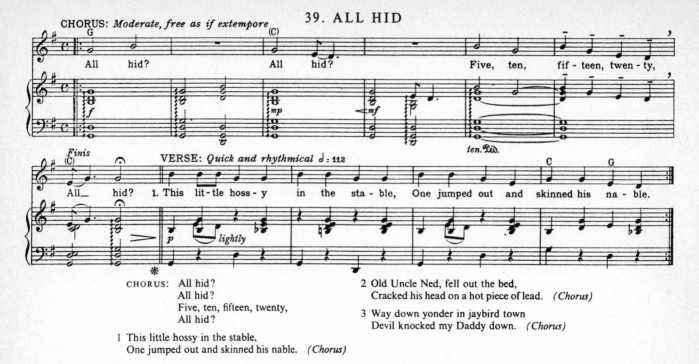

CHORUS: All hid?
        All hid?
        Five, ten, fifteen, twenty,
        All hid?

1 This little hossy in the stable,
  One jumped out and skinned his nable. *(Chorus)*

2 Old Uncle Ned, fell out the bed,
  Cracked his head on a hot piece of lead. *(Chorus)*

3 Way down yonder in jaybird town
  Devil knocked my Daddy down. *(Chorus)*

When the rhymes and games of the American children are put together in one book, the most original chapter will be that of Negro children of the deep South. 'All Hid' is a hide-and-go-seek rhyme known in Mississippi and Alabama, recorded by us in numerous versions for the Library of Congress.

40. RUN, BOYS, RUN

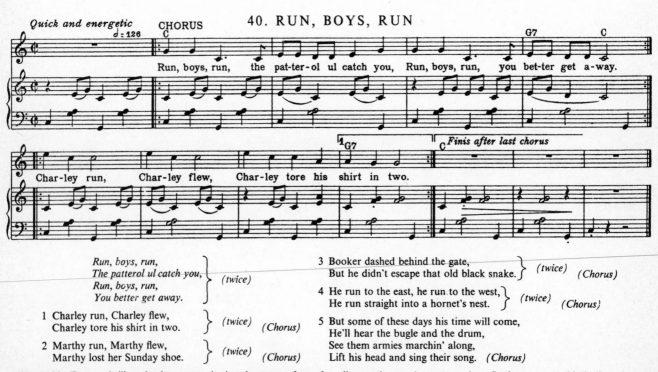

Run, boys, run,
The patterol ul catch you,   *(twice)*
Run, boys, run,
You better get away.

1 Charley run, Charley flew,   *(twice)* *(Chorus)*
  Charley tore his shirt in two.

2 Marthy run, Marthy flew,   *(twice)* *(Chorus)*
  Marthy lost her Sunday shoe.

3 Booker dashed behind the gate,   *(twice)* *(Chorus)*
  But he didn't escape that old black snake.

4 He run to the east, he run to the west, *(twice)* *(Chorus)*
  He run straight into a hornet's nest.

5 But some of these days his time will come,
  He'll hear the bugle and the drum,
  See them armies marchin' along,
  Lift his head and sing their song. *(Chorus)*

After the Nat Turner rebellion, the slave owners instituted a system of armed patrols. Any slave caught off his plantation after dark without a signed pass from his master was liable to be whipped. Since slaves often stole away to see their sweethearts or wives on other plantations, they frequently had to slip past the patrols or outrun them. So there grew up this liveliest of plantation reels, based on the Scots air *Fire on the Mountain*, and sung at slave dances all across the South.

41. FROG WENT A-COURTIN'

1 Frog went a-courtin' an' he did ride,
Um-hum,
Frog went a-courtin' an' he did ride
Sword and pistol by his side,
Um-hum, um-hum.

2 He rode till he came to the mouse's den, *(twice)*
Says, 'Miss Mouse, are you within?' *etc.*

3 He took Miss Mousie on his knee, *(twice)*
An' says, 'Miss Mouse, will you marry me?' *etc.*

4 'Without my uncle Rat's consent, *(twice)*
I wouldn't marry the Pres-i-dent.' *etc.*

5 Uncle Rat came ridin' home, *(twice)*
Says, 'Who's been here since I been gone?' *etc.*

6 Uncle Rat laughed till he shook his sides *(twice)*
To think his niece would be a bride. *etc.*

7 'What will the wedding supper be?' *(twice)*
'Two blue beans and a black-eyed pea'. *etc.*

8 The first that came was a little black bug, *(twice)*
And he fell into the whiskey jug. *etc.*

9 The next that came was a gartersnake, *(twice)*
And coiled himself round the wedding cake. *etc.*

The list of guests can be prolonged until the singer runs out of rhymes.

10 The last to come was an old Tom Cat *(twice)*
Who ate Miss Mouse and Uncle Rat. *etc.*

11 Mister Frog jumped into a lake *(twice)*
And there was swallowed by a big black snake. *etc.*

12 The big black snake, he swum to land *(twice)*
And there was killed by a colored man. *etc.*

13 The colored man he went to France *(twice)*
To teach the ladies how to dance. *etc.*

14 The old hymn book lies on the shelf *(twice)*
If you want any more you can sing it yourself. *etc.*

The sixteenth-century British ballad, *The Frog's Courtship*, has always been America's favourite children's song. It has turned up in scores of versions in every part of the country; this Texas variant, out of my own childhood, has one of the standard tunes, and a text to which American singers have added much.

42. UNCLE REUBEN

1 Raccoon has a bushy tail,
  Possum's tail is bare,
  Rabbit's got no tail at all,
  But a little bunch of hair.
      Uncle Reuben's got the coon and gone, chick-a-chick,
      Done gone, chick-a-chick, done gone, chick-a-chick,
      Uncle Reuben's got the coon and gone, chick-a-chick,
      And left me here behind.

2 Possum up a 'simmon tree,
  Raccoon on the ground,
  Raccoon say to the possum, 'Son,
  Shake them 'simmons down.' *(Chorus)*

3 I met the possum in the road,
  Ask him where he's gwine,
  He 'lowed it was his business
  And never none of mine. *(Chorus)*

4 The possum is a cunning thing,
  He travels after dark,
  Nothing at all disturbs his mind,
  Till he hears old Ranger bark. *(Chorus)*

5 I met a rabbit in the road,
  Ax him whar he's gwine,
  'I ain't got the time to tell you now,
  The old grey hound's behin'.' *(Chorus)*

Southern plantation owners lived in constant fear of slave revolts, and any hint of rebellion or longing for freedom was met with quick and severe punishment. The slave, therefore, learned to speak and sing in a veiled language of double significance. The Biblical stories of the spirituals spoke of his aspirations for freedom and human dignity. The chief actors in his satires on his master became Brer Fox (the master) and timid, big-eyed, clever Brer Rabbit (the slave). The gay verses of his plantation dance songs told of his own experiences disguised as Brer Coon, Brer Possum, or Brer Rabbit. These were the commonest game animals of the South and an important extra in the sometimes scanty rations of the slave. Perhaps these little verses functioned as charms or hunting songs for Negro hunters, often removed by no more than a generation from African animistic beliefs.

43. BLUE-TAIL FLY

1 When I was young I used to wait
On massa, and hand him the plate,
And pass the bottle when he got dry,
And brush away the blue-tail fly.
    Jimmie, crack corn, and I don't care,
    Jimmie, crack corn, and I don't care,
    Jimmie, crack corn, and I don't care,
    My massa's gone away.

2 And when he'd ride in the arternoon,
I'd follow after with a hickory broom,
The pony being very shy,
When bitten by the blue-tail fly. *(Chorus)*

3 One day while riding round the farm,
The flies so numerous they did swarm,
One chanced to bite him on the thigh,
The devil take the blue-tail fly. *(Chorus)*

4 The pony ran, he jump, he kick,
He throwed old massa in the ditch,
He died and the jury wondered why,
The verdick was – the blue-tail fly. *(Chorus)*

The history of this little ballad is that of so many of the best of the black-face minstrel songs. The refrain, a genuine bit of plantation song, was picked up by the abolitionist composer, John Work, and made into a song which became a favourite of many Unionists, among them Abraham Lincoln. Then the song passed back into folk currency among Negroes. Professor Dorothy Scarborough discovered this version in Louisiana in the 1920s; I found it in her book, taught it to the Golden Gate Quartet and to Burl Ives, who made it again into one of America's best loved songs.

44. GREEN CORN

CHORUS 1: *Green corn, come along Charley,*
Green corn, gwine ta tell Polly,
Green corn, green corn.
1 All I want in this creation,
Pretty little wife and a big plantation,
Green corn, green corn. *(Chorus 1)*

2 Two little boys to call me pappy,
One name Sop and the other name Gravy,
Green corn, green corn. *(Chorus 1)*

3 One name Sop and the other name Gravy,
One gonna put up and the other gonna save it,
Green corn, green corn. *(Chorus 1)*

CHORUS 2: *Stand around, stand around the jimmyjohn,*
Stand around, stand around the jimmyjohn,
Stand around, stand around.
(Chorus 1)

At a very early date Negro slave musicians played the dance music for plantation balls. Soon they introduced their own primitive stringed instrument, the banjo, which became the companion of the European fiddle at square dances. Negro variants and imitations of white dance tunes came into existence and presently hybrid tunes evolved, which were neither white nor black, but simply Southern. Such a slavery-time Negro reel is this Louisiana dance tune, which we collected from Leadbelly.

45. WE'RE GONNA RAISE A RUKUS

1 My ol' massa say to me,
  Raise a rukus tonight,
  'When I die, gonna set you free,'
  Raise a rukus tonight.
  Lived so long till his head got bald,
  Raise a rukus tonight,
  Got out the notion of dyin' at all,
  Raise a rukus tonight.
      Come along, little children, come along,
      While the moon is shinin' bright, shinin' bright,
      Get on board, down the river flow,
      We gonna raise a rukus tonight.

2 Now there's ol' massa lyin' in the leaves,
  Head full of lice and clothes full of fleas.
  But when ol' missy gets to blowin' her horn,
  There goes Sambo a-hillin' up the corn. *(Chorus)*

3 Went to the river to be baptized,
  Stepped on a root and I got capsized,
  The water was deep and the preacher was weak,
  This sinner went to Heaven from the bottom of the creek. *(Chorus)*

4 Great black man a-lyin' on a log,
  Hand on his gun, eye on a hog,
  Gun says 'boom', hog says 'bip',
  Black man on him with all of his grip. *(Chorus)*

5 Some folk say the preacher won't steal,
  But I caught two in my cornfield,
  One had a bushel, the other had a peck,
  With two big roas'n'-ears round his neck. *(Chorus)*

6 If you want to go to Heaven, here's what you do,
  Stick your feet in mutton stew,
  Devil try to grab with his red-hot hand,
  You ooze right into the promised land. *(Chorus)*

The first original development in American entertainment music was the minstrel show. There white professionals blackened their faces and sang the 'plantation' songs which gave the comfortable impression that Negroes were a contented, lazy, carefree lot, who wept when their white masters died. A certain amount of genuine Negro rhythm and wit percolated into this genre, and its popularity endured for a hundred years. Some minstrel songs containing racial caricatures passed for genuine and were accepted by folk Negroes. Out of these songs again developed minstrel pieces, in which the white man and his culture became the object of satire. Such a song is this joyful, ragtime tune, the top favourite of rural Negro quartets in the thirties. We recorded it in Texas in 1933.

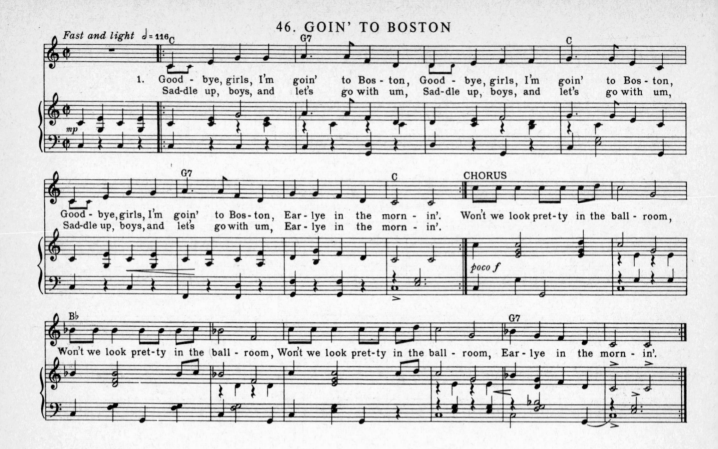

Fast and light ♩=116

1. Good - bye, girls, I'm goin' to Bos - ton, Good - bye, girls, I'm goin' to Bos - ton,
   Sad - dle up, boys, and let's go with um, Sad - dle up, boys, and let's go with um,

Good - bye, girls, I'm goin' to Bos - ton, Ear - lye in the morn - in'. Won't we look pret - ty in the ball - room,
Sad - dle up, boys, and let's go with um, Ear - lye in the morn - in'.

Won't we look pret - ty in the ball - room, Won't we look pret - ty in the ball - room, Ear - lye in the morn - in'.

1 Goodbye, girls, I'm goin' to Boston, *(three times)*
  Earlye in the mornin'.
  Saddle up, boys, and let's go with um, *(three times)*
  Earlye in the mornin'.
  Won't we look pretty in the ballroom, (three times)
  Earlye in the mornin'.

2 Out of the way, you'll get run over, *(three times)*
  Earlye in the mornin'.
  Rights and lefts to make it better, *(three times)*
  Earlye in the mornin'. *(Chorus)*

3 Swing your partner all the way to Boston, *(three times)*
  Earlye in the mornin'.
  Johnny, Johnny, gonna tell your pappy, *(three times)*
  Earlye in the mornin'. *(Chorus)*

The strict religious folk of the frontier regarded the fiddle as an instrument of the devil, and the square dance as a stepping stone on the road to hell. Barred from dancing, the young people held play parties where the courtly children's games of the past were played and sung by adults, and where other sung-dances, called play-party games, were invented. Although they closely resembled the forbidden square dances, they were held to be innocent so long as all the music was vocal and the dancers didn't cross their feet or swing the girls while dancing. (Recorded from the singing of Jean Ritchie in 1948.)

47. WEEVILY WHEAT

Quick and vigorous, in hoe-down style ♩ = 108

1. I don't want none of your wee-vil-y wheat An' I don't want none o' your bar-ley, Take some flour in half an hour An' bake a cake for Char-ley. O Char-ley, he's a nice young man, An' Char-ley he's a dan-dy, Ever-y time he goes to town He brings the girls some can-dy. 2. The *etc.* can-dy.

1 I don't want none of your weevily wheat
   An' I don't want none o' your barley,
   Take some flour in half an hour
   An' bake a cake for Charley.
     O Charley, he's a nice young man,
     An' Charley he's a dandy,
     Every time he goes to town
     He brings the girls some candy.

2 The higher up the cherry tree
  The riper grows the cherry,
  The sooner th'at you court a gal
  The sooner she will marry. *(Chorus)*

3 Take her by her lilywhite hand
  And lead her like a pigeon,
  Make her dance the weevily wheat
  And scatter her religion. *(Chorus)*

4 Charley here and Charley there
  And Charley over the ocean,
  Charley, he'll come back some day
  If he don't change his notion. *(Chorus)*

Dancing to instrumental accompaniment was also frowned upon by respect-able people in frontier Texas, Oklahoma, and the Middle West. There the sung 'play party', led by cowboy prompters, developed mightily, slowly re-introducing the old square-dance steps into the respectable game songs. One of the favourite western 'plays' was this American variant of the Scots *Over the Water to Charlie*, this adaptation by John A. Lomax.

48. BILLY BOY

Moderately fast ♩ = 120

1. 'O where have you been, Bil-ly boy, Bil-ly boy, O__ where have you been, charm-ing Bil-ly?' 'I've been to see my wife, she's the charm of my life, She's a young thing and can-not leave her mam-my.' 2. 'Did she *etc.*

1 'O where have you been, Billy boy, Billy boy,
O where have you been, charming Billy?'
'I've been to see my wife, she's the charm of my life,
She's a young thing and cannot leave her mammy.'

2 'Did she ask you in,' *etc.*
'Yes, she asked me in,
And she bit me on the chin,' *etc.*

3 'Did she take your hat?' *etc.*
'Yes, she took my hat
And she threw it at the cat,' *etc.*

4 'How old is she?' *etc.*
'Twice six, twice seven,
Forty-eight and eleven,' *etc.*

5 'How tall is she?' *etc.*
'She's tall as a pine
And straight as punkin vine,' *etc.*

6 'Can she bake a cherry pie?' *etc.*
'She can bake a cherry pie,
Quick as a cat can wink its eye,' *etc.*

7 'Can she make a pair of britches?' *etc.*
'Yes, she can make a pair of britches,
Quick as you can count the stitches,' *etc.*

8 'Did she sit close to you?' *etc.*
'Yes, she sat as close to me
As the bark upon the tree,' *etc.*

9 'Is she fitted for your wife?' *etc.*
'Yes, she's fitted for my wife
As my pocket for my knife,' *etc.*

The lilting 6/8 rhythm of the north of England question and answer piece became a drawling 2/4 on the lips of American singers. Its gaiety took on an ironic tall-story quality, and in this form it became a universal pioneer favourite, found among rural singers in every state of the Union. This is the Texas version as sung by the Lomax family.

49. GET ALONG HOME, CINDY

1 Cindy is a pretty girl,
  She comes from the South,
  She's so sweet the honey-bees
  Swarm around her mouth.
      Get along home,
      Get along home,
      Get along home, Cindy, Cindy,
      I'll marry you some day.

2 She told me that she loved me,
  She called me sugar-plum,
  She flang her arms around me
  And I thought my time had come. *(Chorus)*

3 Cindy went to the meetin',
  She shouted and she sung,
  She got so full of glory
  She shook her stockings down. *(Chorus)*

4 Cindy got religion,
  She'd had it once before,
  But when she heard my old banjo
  She was the first one on the floor. *(Chorus)*

5 Preacher in the pulpit
  Preachin' mighty bold,
  Preachin' for the money
  To save the sinner's soul. *(Chorus)*

6 I went down to Cindy's house,
  Cindy wasn't at home,
  I set down in Cindy's chair
  And rocked until she come. *(Chorus)*

7 I went to see my Cindy,
  Carried a pair of shoes,
  Asked her if she'd marry me,
  She said she couldn't refuse. *(Chorus)*

8 I wish I had a needle,
  As fine as I could sew,
  I'd sew that gal to my coat-tail
  And down the road I'd go. *(Chorus)*

Cindy is derived from the black-face minstrel song, *Cindy Lou*, but reached its present shape among mountain square-dance musicians who added scores of rollicking verses in the tradition of Celtic mouth music. Recorded in Kentucky in 1933, with verses from other mountain states.

50. OLD JOE CLARK

1 Old Joe Clark he had a house,
   Forty storeys high,
   And every storey in that house
   Was lined with chicken pie.
   CHORUS 1: *Fare you well, old Joe Clark,*
              Fare you well, I say,
              Fare you well, old Joe Clark,
              For I'm a-goin' away.

2 Old Joe Clark he had a dog,
   Blind as he could be,
   Run a possum up a holler log,
   You'd swear that dog could see. *(Chorus 1)*

3 I went down to old Joe's house,
   Old Joe wasn't at home,
   Jumped in bed with old Joe's wife,
   And broke her tuckin' comb. *(Chorus 1)*

4 I went down to Lexington,
   Didn't know the route,
   Put me in a coffee pot
   And poured me out the spout. *(Chorus 1)*

5 Met a possum in the road,
   Mean as he could be,
   Jumped the fence and whipped my dog,
   And bristled up at me. *(Chorus 1)*

6 I wish I was an apple,
   Hangin' on a tree,
   Every time that pretty gal passed
   She'd take a bite of me. *(Chorus 1)*

7 I wish I had a lariat rope,
   Long as I could throw,
   Throw it round my sweetheart's waist
   And down the road we'd go.
   CHORUS 2: *Round and round, old Joe Clark,*
              Round and round I say,
              He'll follow me a thousand miles
              To hear my banjo play.

8 I wish I had a muley cow,
   Corn to feed it on,
   Pretty little girl to stay at home
   And feed it while I'm gone. *(Chorus 2)*

9 Peaches in the summertime,
   Apples in the fall,
   If I can't get the girl I want,
   I won't have none at all. *(Chorus 2)*

10 Old Joe Clark, he's killed a man,
   Throwed him in the branch,
   Now old Joe's a-goin' to hang,
   Ain't no other chance. *(Chorus 2)*

11 Never got no money,
   Got no place to stay,
   Got no place to lay my head,
   And th' chicken's a-crowin' for day.
   CHORUS 3: *Fare you well, old Joe Clark,*
              Fare you well, goodbye,
              Fare you well, old Joe Clark,
              For I hate to see you die.

I have heard it said that Joe Clark made mountain moonshine in the Blue Ridge Mountains of Virginia, but no one can be certain who he actually was. However, as hero of Oklahoma's favourite play party song, set to America's catchiest square-dance tune, he became a prime object of our love of crazy, exaggerated humour, and his name and reputation will never die till the last square-dance fiddle tune has been played. We recorded this tune in Kentucky in 1933.

51. BLACK-EYED SUSIE

1 Black-eyed Susie's about half grown,
   She jumps on the boys like a dog on a bone.
   It's hey, pretty little black-eyed Susie,
   Hey, pretty little black-eyed Susie,
   Hey, hey, hey.

2 'Say, old man, I want your daughter,
   To split my wood and carry my water.' *(Chorus)*

3 'Say, young man, you can take her if you want her,
   All I want is a dollar and a quarter.' *(Chorus)*

4 Black-eyed Susie's a sunburnt daisy,
   If I don't get her I'm going crazy. *(Chorus)*

5 I asked Susie to be my wife,
   And she come at me with a barlow knife. *(Chorus)*

6 Black-eyed Susie went huckleberry pickin',
   Susie got kissed and the boys took a lickin'. *(Chorus)*

Occasionally quite bawdy, this lilting American mouth music has long been popular at square-dances and play parties, from the Smoky mountains to the Panhandle. It makes an excellent fiddle tune, but when there is no fiddler handy a good singer can give the precise beat for a buck and wing dance by ranting *Black-eyed Susie*. We recorded it in Harlan County, Kentucky, in 1933.

52. SOURWOOD MOUNTAIN

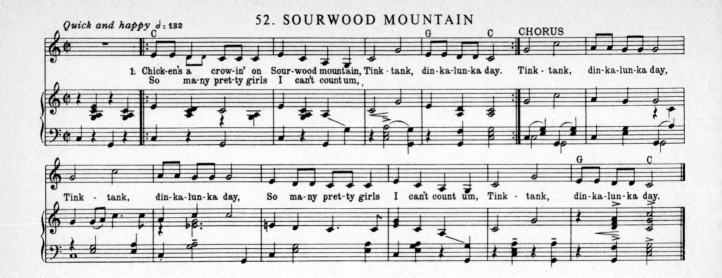

1 Chicken's a-crowin' on Sourwood mountain,
Tink-tank, dinka-lunka day,
So many pretty girls I can't count um,
Tink-tank, dinka-lunka day.
Tink-tank, dinka-lunka day, (twice)
So many pretty girls I can't count um,
Tink-tank, dinka-lunka day.

2 I got a gal at the head of the holler, *etc.*
She won't come and I won't foller, *etc.* *(Chorus)*

3 I got a gal across the river, *etc.*
Two more jumps and I'll be with her, *etc.* *(Chorus)*

4 Big dog bark and little one bite you, *etc.*
Big gal court you, the little un fight you, *etc.* *(Chorus)*

During the pioneer period, the fiddle was the principal instrument of the American folk. Where it was not banned for religious reasons, it provided the music for pioneer square-dances – livelier folk variants of the statelier country dances of Britain. American fiddlers kept alive many British airs, but also developed hundreds of American tunes in a virile, highly rhythmic style of their own, with comic verses to match. One of the Southern mountain classics is this tribute to 'the gals on Sourwood Mountain'.

IV

Spirituals and Work Songs

IV. SPIRITUALS AND WORK SONGS

AN often quoted critic of early New England remarked that a congregation of psalm-singing Puritans sounded like a concert of braying jackasses. There is a grain of objective truth in his observation – the colonial settlers, like almost any assembly of Anglo-American whites in our time, folk or sophisticated, sang poorly in chorus. Their voices did not blend; their improvised harmony, if any, did not come off; their unison was ragged.

It is probable that this captious New England critic was describing a *surge* song, a type once fashionable on the whole frontier and still in vogue in some churches in the west of Scotland and the Southern States. Surge-singing was an expedient often adopted when hymn-books were rare and/or illiteracy was the norm. The deacon (precentor) intoned the first line or two of the psalm, outlining the familiar tune, then led the whole congregation through the same passage at a slower tempo. In white congregations, it must be admitted, there were many who trailed sadly in the rear, took the wrong pitch and had to begin afresh or sing their own versions of the tune. Undaunted, the deacon gave out two more lines but, the next time through perhaps, slowed the tempo again, so that the rearguard could catch up.

After a century or more of this treatment, the originally lively Puritan tunes became dragged out and dreary fossils; yet the force of religious custom was so strong that it took a revolution to replace them. G. P. Jackson, in his many excellent books on the history of the white spiritual, has told the story in full detail. In sum, the American Revolution overthrew the power of the established churches and the people took control of their religious music. Sophisticated composers with their allies, the country singing masters, introduced rural America to the pleasant custom of fuguing tunes and of singing in four or five parts. Frontier folk ministers of radical Methodist and Baptist persuasions whipped their huge congregations into religious hysteria by leading them in 'new' hymns, which were set to sensual and rhythmic secular folk tunes of every sort.

In using 'the devil's tunes' for the Lord's work, the Wesleys and others set a precedent that modern Holy Rollers follow today, when they put sacred texts to jazzy tunes so their congregation 'can get happy and dance for the Lord'. The hymn books of many American Protestant sects contain the approved and fossilized remains of various phases of this developing folk hymnology.

Since the pioneer Protestant church regarded the singing of 'worldly' ditties as an offence for which the singer might be 'churched' (that is, tried and possibly dismissed from the congregation), a great number of religious songs were needed to satisfy the musical appetite of the song-hungry frontier; something like half of America's folk-song repertory was religious, and the proportion of sacred to profane was probably higher among the Negroes.

The slaves found in the evangelical Protestant church an institution perfectly adapted to their cultural needs. On the doctrinal side, they were promised rewards in glory in recompense for the compliant suffering on this earth; Hell yawned wide at the feet of their oppressors; Christ promised to forgive them for the sins their situation forced upon them. A communal and democratic style of worship allowed them to express their solidarity and their inherited need for group activity – to pray, to sing as one voice, even to dance together.

On the whole the South favoured the conversion of the slaves. Where religious meetings were forbidden, the slaves prayed and sang in secret. They continued their African dance form, shuffling in single file and in a counter-clockwise direction round their meeting-houses, chanting in their African leader-chorus style and becoming possessed (getting 'happy'), just as their African ancestors had done. To the worn-out surge-songs they brought their African talent for choral polyphony, so that a sound arose like a mighty organ playing in the darkness of the South. Their spirituals, in which they personalized God and the Devil and identified themselves with the woeful children of Israel, were touched with the charm and poignancy of primitive poetry. When the black regiments of freed slaves marched into battle on the Union side, these freedom songs thundered across the field.

The creation of Negro spirituals has never ceased from that day to this. In ballads, in musical sermons, in quartet songs, in Holy Roller chants, in the recent Gospel style, the religious Negro has developed style after style – each with scores of well-nigh perfect songs. If you were to ask a Southern congregation today to render the antebellum spirituals included in this volume, they would have to look them up in their hymn books.

Singing at work was regarded by most Southern masters as a harmless, if not actually helpful form of community activity. The chants of labour kept the black man contented and diverted during his long days of toil, and a lively, steady rhythm moulded a group of Negroes into a more efficient machine. On many jobs, work song leaders were employed who had no other duty but to sing, and so there arose a great body of functional songs, at least the equal of the spirituals in number and interest.

Unfortunately, the church, which was the only stable institution in the Negro community, condemned work songs as 'worldly and sinful', and so, as the machine replaced group labour and work songs lost their function, most of them disappeared. The prison work songs must stand, therefore, for the paddling songs, the corn-husking songs, the rice-pounding songs, the longshoremen's chants which once livened and humanized the cruel labours of the Southern frontier.

53. LITTLE DAVID

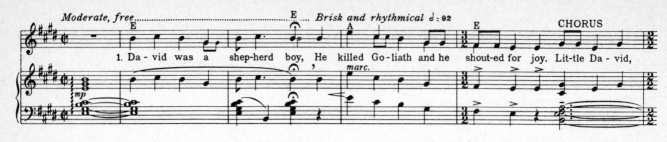

1 David was a shepherd boy,
  He killed Goliath and he shouted for joy.
  Little David, play on your harp,
  Hallelu! Hallelu!
  Little David, play on your harp,
  Hallelu!

2 Tell you what little David done,
  Picked up a rock and out he run. *(Chorus)*

3 Goliath was a mighty man,
  But God put strength in David's hand. *(Chorus)*

4 Goliath swung his iron sword,
  But David hit him with the power of God. *(Chorus)*

5 Watch the sun, how steady she run,
  Don't never let it catch you with your work undone. *(Chorus)*

David, Moses, Daniel, and Joshua – the Hebrew leaders, who fought against great odds for the freedom of their people, became the heroes of the religious Negro. Inspired rural preachers wove wonderful rhapsodic sermons about the lives of these biblical figures, touching the stark biblical accounts with folk fantasy. For the Southern Negro, these ancient Israelites were symbols of their own aspirations for liberty, and, as they sang about them, they got 'happy' and shouted all over the church. (Adapted by A. Lomax)

54. THE CHERRY TREE CAROL

1 Mary and Joseph were walking one day,
   In a garden of cherries they happened to stray,
   In a garden of cherries they chanced for to stray.

2 Mary spoke to Joseph, so meek and so mild,
   'Go gather me some cherries, for I am with child.' *(twice)*

3 Joseph flew in angry, in angry flew he,
   'Let the father of your baby gather cherries for thee.' *(twice)*

4 Then Jesus, he spoke up from his mother's womb,
   'Bow low down, cherry tree, bow low to the ground.' *(twice)*

5 Then the cherry trees bowed down, bowed low to the ground,
   And Mary gathered cherries while Joseph stood around. *(twice)*

6 Then Joseph took Mary all on his right knee,
   Said, 'Tell me, pretty baby, when your birthday shall be.' *(twice)*

7 'On the sixth day of January my birthday shall be,
   When the elements shall tremble and the stars shall dance with glee.' *(twice)*

This British carol is based on popular medieval stories derived from the pseudo-Matthew Gospel, in which Joseph has doubts of Mary's fidelity. American singers favour the ending in which the unborn baby predicts that *Old Christmas* will be his birthday. I have heard singers name 5, 6, and 7 January. All these dates were correct, but in different epochs. Old Christmas did fall on 5 January until 1779, when one day was dropped from the Calendar, and on 6 January until 1900, when another day was dropped and it became 7 January. Whatever date they favoured, all backwoods singers believed that on Old Christmas the cattle in their stalls would fall upon their knees and speak about the birth of Jesus.

55. POOR WAYFARING STRANGER

I am a poor wayfaring stranger,
Traveling through this world of woe,
And there's no sickness, toil or danger
In that bright land to which I go.
I'm goin' there to meet my mother,
I'm goin' there no more to roam,
I'm just a-goin' over Jordan,
I'm just a-goin' over home.

(The song continues through 'father', 'sister', 'brother', etc.)

The American revolution set the American pioneer free from the dominating and tyrannical influence of the established churches of the eastern seaboard. A great revival movement, directed by Baptist and Methodist itinerant preachers, kept the West and South in a state of religious excitement for several generations. Thousands of spirituals and revival hymns were composed during this period, some using secular folk tunes, others communally sung together during the meetings, and still others written by circuit-riding preachers and itinerant singing teachers. These white spirituals bear an intimate relationship to the Negro spirituals which were created at about the same time.

56. HEBREW CHILDREN

1 Where, O where, are the Hebrew children?
Where, O where, are the Hebrew children?
Where, O where, are the Hebrew children?
Safe over in the promised land.
Though the furnace flamed around them,
God while in their troubles found them,
He with love and mercy bound them
Safe over in the promised land.

2 Where, O where, are the twelve apostles? *(three times)*
Safe over in the promised land.
They went up through pain and sighing,
Scoffing, scourging, crucifying,
Nobly for their master dying,
Safe over in the promised land.

3 Where, O where, are the holy Christians? *(three times)*
Safe over in the promised land.
Those who've washed their robes and made them
White and spotless, pure, and laid them
Where no earthly stain can fade them,
Safe over in the promised land.

4 Where, O where, are the good old patriarchs? *(three times)*
Safe over in the promised land.
By and by we will go and meet them *(three times)*
Way over in the promised land.

5 Where, O where, is good old Shadrach?
Where, O where, is good old Meshach?
Where, O where, is good old Abednego?
Way over in the promised land.
They went through the fiery furnace *(three times)*
Safe over in the promised land.

(Indian Song from Missouri)

6 Clo me sal sal mit a Moses *(three times)*
Hiclo piclo peace in-e-ay,
Clati-clati-wamp pit-e-i- pit-e-i-wa *(twice)*
Clati-clati-wamp pit-e-as-so by-way,
Hico piclo peace in-e-ay

Clo me sal sal mit a Daniel, *etc.*

When the Baptists and the Methodist revivals swept the frontier between the 1780s and the 1830s, large numbers of people gathered in improvised meeting houses in the wilderness, where they were addressed by 'hell-fire' preachers and where they prayed and sung themselves into a state of ecstasy. They wept, shouted, danced, rolled on the ground, climbed trees, went into trances, saw visions – always they sang vigorous rhythmic spirituals. These 'white spirituals' were undoubtedly influenced by the Negroes present in the congregations; they were also imitated by Negroes in their own revivals. Among the favourite white spiritual tunes was this song, attributed to Rev. Peter Cartwright, who was born in Virginia in 1785 and died in 1872 in Illinois, after singing it wherever he conducted his camp meetings.

57. NOBODY KNOWS THE TROUBLE I SEE

CHORUS: *Nobody knows the trouble I see,*
Nobody knows like Jesus,
Nobody knows the trouble I see,
O yes, Lord.

1 Sometimes I'm up, sometimes I'm down,
O yes, Lord,
Sometimes I'm almost to the ground,
O yes, Lord. *(Chorus)*

2 Now you may see me goin' 'long so,
O yes, Lord,
But I have tri-als here below,
O yes, Lord. *(Chorus)*

Although many slave spirituals took their start from the folk hymns of the whites, the qualities that gave them universal appeal were Negro. They are magnificent group songs, composed by a people having all the special African skills in singing and improvising in chorus. They reflect the African's intimate and personalized attitudes to celestial affairs. Most of all, they poignantly express the emotions of an enslaved people. In the official Southern view, if not always in practice, the Negro slave was regarded as no better than an animal. When it was convenient and profitable, slave families were broken up, mothers were sold away from their children and wives from their husbands. After 'freedom', the Negro was left to shift for himself, without land or place or roots. Out of such experiences came this lament, one of the most deeply moving of songs.

58. DIDN'T MY LORD DELIVER DANIEL

Strongly marked, vigorous ♩=69

CHORUS: *Didn't my Lord deliver Da-nu-el,*
Da-nu-el, Da-nu-el,
Didn't my Lord deliver Da-nu-el,
And why not every man?

1 He delivered Daniel from the lion's den,
And Jonah from the belly of the whale,
And the Hebrew children from the fiery furnace,
So why not every man? *(Chorus)*

2 The wind blows east, the wind blows west,
It blows like judgement day,
And ev'ry soul that never did pray,
Will be glad to pray that day. *(Chorus)*

3 The moon run down in a purple stream,
The sun refuse to shine,
And every star will disappear,
King Jesus will be mine. *(Chorus)*

This genuine antebellum spiritual, one of the most powerful freedom songs in any language, should be sung with strong rhythm and great drive. Its apocalyptic vision of judgement day, perfectly acceptable in a religious context to Southern Protestant slave holders, certainly comforted the slave by assuring him that God in his own time would punish the wicked and cruel and succour his innocent and suffering people. For the Negro slave his spirituals carried a double symbolism – redemption from sin and freedom from servitude.

81

59. GO DOWN, MOSES

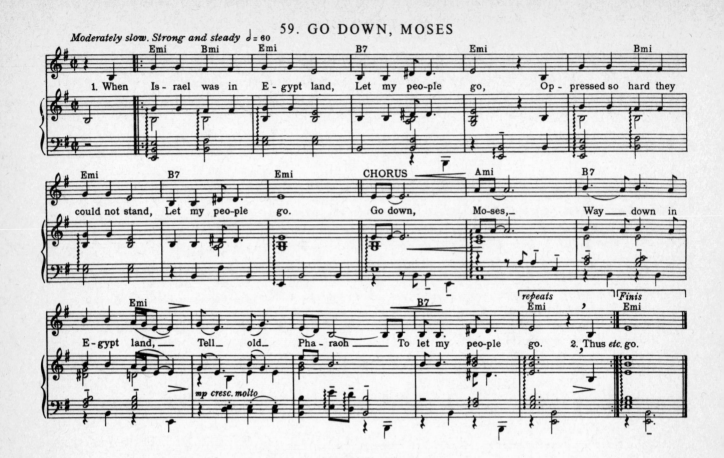

1 When Israel was in Egypt land,
Let my people go,
Oppressed so hard they could not stand,
Let my people go.
Go down, Moses,
Way down in Egypt land,
Tell old Pharaoh
To let my people go.

2 'Thus spoke the Lord' bold Moses said,
'Let my people go,
If not, I'll smite your first-born dead,
Let my people go.' *(Chorus)*

3 'Your foes shall not before you stand,
Let my people go,
And you'll possess fair Canaan's land,
Let my people go.' *(Chorus)*

4 'You'll not get lost in the wilderness,
Let my people go,
With a lighted candle in your breast,
Let my people go.' *(Chorus)*

This famous freedom spiritual of the Negro slaves is said to refer to Harriet Tubman, an escaped slave, who returned time after time into the South to lead bands of her people to freedom over the underground railroad. In the editor's opinion it is the finest of American folk songs.

60. GREAT DAY

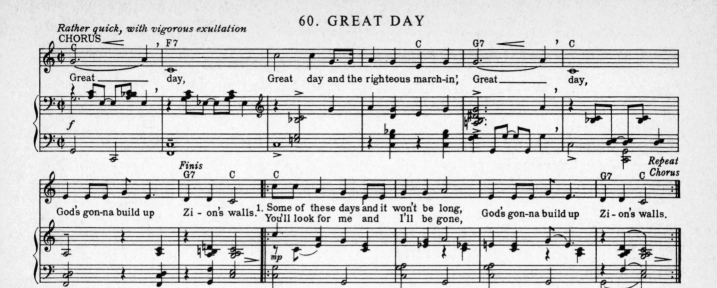

CHORUS: *Great day,*
Great day and the righteous marchin',
Great day,
God's gonna build up Zion's walls.

1 Some of these days and it won't be long,
  God's gonna build up Zion's walls,
  You'll look for me and I'll be gone,
  God's gonna build up Zion's walls. *(Chorus)*

2 Well, up on the mountain Jehovah he spoke,
  Out of his mouth came fire and smoke. *(Chorus)*

3 I know my God's a man of war,
  He fit that battle at Jericho's walls. *(Chorus)*

4 My God gave Noah the rainbow sign,
  'No more water but fire next time.' *(Chorus)*

5 One of these mornin's, bright and fair,
  Gonna hitch on my wings and try the air. *(Chorus)*

6 Away up in heaven I'm gonna shout,
  Nobody there to put me out. *(Chorus)*

7 O Hell is deep and Hell is wide,
  Hell ain't got no bottom or side. *(Chorus)*

8 I'd rather pray myself away,
  Than live and burn in Hell one day. *(Chorus)*

This spiritual, with its echoes of emancipation, was the kind that followed a powerful revival sermon and stirred the church members into religious hysteria. The verses portray the Lord, and Heaven and Hell, as they appeared to the fancy of the folk Negro in the old South.

61. WHAT MONTH WAS JESUS BORN IN?

1 What month was Jesus born in?
Ref: Last month in the year.
What month was Jesus born in?
Ref: Last month in the year.
　　　Oo–Lawd, you got January, February, March,
　　　Oo–Lawd, you got April, May and June,
　　　You got July, August, September,
　　　October and-a November,
　　　You got the Twenty-fifth day of December,
　　　You got the last month in the year.

2 He was born of a virgin mother, *etc.* *(Chorus)*

3 He was laid in an oxen manger, *etc.* *(Chorus)*

4 His mother's name was Mary, *etc.* *(Chorus)*

On Christmas Eve the Negro slaves held a 'watch night' service in which they prayed and sang until midnight, and then rejoiced in the anniversary of the birth of Jesus. During these watch nights many Negro carols were created, and none more beautiful than this Alabama spiritual, only recently discovered. It may, indeed, be quite a new song, for spirituals are still being made; yet it conforms so perfectly to the tradition that it is impossible to date.

62. DOWN BY THE RIVERSIDE

Guitarists may capo up and play the chords in brackets.

1 I'm goin' to lay down my heavy load,
Down by the riverside,
Down by the riverside,
Down by the riverside,
I'm goin' to lay down my heavy load
Down by the riverside,
I ain't a-gonna study war no more.
I ain't a-gonna study war no more. (four times)

2 I'm goin' to lay down my sword and shield, *etc. (Chorus)*

3 I'm goin' to put on my travelin' shoes, *etc. (Chorus)*

4 I'm goin' to put on my long white robe, *etc. (Chorus)*

5 I'm goin' to put on my starry crown, *etc. (Chorus)*

A rousing hallelujah spiritual that has made many a sinner shout in church, this song also served as a drill march for Negro regiments in the Second World War, and it sounds fine with a New Orleans jazz band as well.

63. THE BALLAD OF THE BOLL WEEVIL

Moderate jog-trot ♩=132

1. Have you heard the la-test, The la-test of your songs? It's a-bout them lit-tle boll wee-vils, Gon-na rob you of your home. Just a-look-in' for a home, Just a-look-in' for a home.

CHORUS

Just a-look-in' for a home. Just a-look-in' for a home.

Finis

2. The boll etc.

1 Have you heard the latest,
The latest of your songs?
It's about them little boll weevils,
Gonna rob you of your home.
CHORUS 1: *Just a-lookin' for a home,*
Just a-lookin' for a home.

2 The boll weevil is a little black bug,
Come from Mexico, they tell,
Come to eat our cotton up
And raise pertic'ler hell. *(Chorus 1)*

3 The farmer ask the boll weevil,
'What makes your head so red?'
'I've been traveling this wide world over,
It's a wonder I ain't dead.' *(Chorus 1)*

4 The first time I seen the boll weevil,
He was on that western plain,
The next time I seen the boll weevil,
He had hopped that Memphis 'plane.
(Chorus 1)

5 The next time I seen the boll weevil,
He was runnin' a spinnin' wheel,
The last time I seen him,
He was ridin' 'n autymobile. *(Chorus 1)*

6 The farmer says to the merchant,
'I'm in an awful fix.
The boll weevil ate all my cotton up
And left me only sticks.
CHORUS 2: *We got no home,*
We got no home.'

7 The farmer say to the banker,
'I ain't got but one bale,
And before you take that one
I'll suffer and die in jail.
CHORUS 3: *I'll have a home,*
I'll have a home.'

8 Then the farmer taken the boll weevil,
And buried him down in ice,
The boll weevil tell the farmer, 'Lawd,
That's mighty cool and nice.
CHORUS 4: *It is my home,*
Yes, it is my home.'

9 Then the farmer taken the boll weevil
And put him in Paris Green
The boll weevil tell the farmer, 'Lawd,
That's the best I ever seen.
CHORUS 5: *It is my home,*
Lord, it is my home.'

10 Boll weevil say to the lightnin' bug,
'I wish I could be you.
With that little tail-light of yours
I could work the whole night through.
CHORUS 6: *I'll have your home,' (twice)*

11 Boll weevil say to the doctor,
'Better pour out all your pills.
When I get through with the farmer,
He won't pay no doctor bills.
CHORUS 7: *Won't have no home,' (twice)*

12 The merchant got half the cotton,
Boll weevil got the rest,
Didn't leave the poor farmer's wife,
But one old cotton dress.
CHORUS 8: *And it's full of holes. (twice)*

The boll weevil, a tiny parasite which lays its eggs in the budding cotton boll, attacked the Texan cotton fields in the 1890s and gradually spread eastwards towards the Atlantic coast. Before scientists found the means to control it, it had destroyed the one-crop system of the South and driven many people off the land. The Negro farm labourers, set adrift in this rural depression, felt they were no longer wanted or needed anywhere, and in this song they identified themselves with the little *boll weevil*, which the Government experts were trying to drive out of the cotton fields at the time. Both the Negro and the boll weevil were looking for a home. The ballad was first discovered by John Lomax in the early 1900s.

64. THE GREY GOOSE

1. Well, last Sunday mornin',
   Lawd, Lawd, Lawd,
   The preacher went a-huntin',
   Lawd, Lawd, Lawd.

2. He took along his zulu, *etc.*
   And the hound dog, he went, too. *etc.*

3. They got to the big woods, *etc.*
   And along come the grey goose. *etc.*

4. He up to his shoulder, *etc.*
   He up to his shoulder. *etc.*

5. And he ram back the hammer, *etc.*
   Then he pulled on the trigger. *etc.*

6. And the zulu went 'boo-loo', *etc.*
   And the zulu went 'boo-loo'. *etc.*

7. Well, down he come a-windin', *etc.*
   We was six weeks a-findin'. *etc.*

8. So yo' wife and my wife, *etc.*
   They give a feather pickin'. *etc.*

9. He was six weeks a-pickin', *etc.*
   He was six weeks a-pickin'. *etc.*

10. Then they put him on to parboil, *etc.*
    And he was ten days a-parboil. *etc.*

11. And they set him on the table, *etc.*
    And the knife couldn't stick him. *etc.*

12. Then they threw him in the hog-pen, *etc.*
    Then he broke the belly's jawbone. *etc.*

13. So they took him to the saw-mill, *etc.*
    And he bust the saw's teeth out. *etc.*

14. Well, the last time I seed him, *etc.*
    He was flyin' 'cross the ocean. *etc.*

15. Wid a long stream of goslin's, *etc.*
    And they all went 'Quink-quank'. *etc.*

16. He was a hell of a grey goose, *etc.*
    He was a hell of a grey goose. *etc.*

A call-response song of a primitive Afro-American type once common among slaves, this work song epic was in use among Texas Negro prisoners in the thirties. The theme – 'You can't kill me no matter what you try' – was an essential one to the singing convicts as they strove to keep alive in the horrifying conditions of the Southern prison camps.

1 John Henry was a little baby boy,
  You could hold him in the palm of your hand,
  He gave a long and a lonesome cry,
  'Gonna be a steel-drivin' man, Lawd, Lawd,
  Gonna be a steel drivin' man.'

2 They took John Henry to the tunnel,
  Put him in the lead to drive,
  The rock was so tall, John Henry so small,
  That he lied down his hammer and he cried, Lawd, Lawd,
  Lied down his hammer and he cried.

3 John Henry started on the right hand,
  The steam drill started on the left,
  'Fo' I'd let that steamdrill beat me down,
  I'd hammer my fool self to death, Lawd, Lawd,' etc.

4 John Henry told his captain,
  'A man ain't nothin' but a man,
  'Fo' I let your steamdrill beat me down
  I'll die with this hammer in my hand, Lawd, Lawd,' etc.

5 John Henry had a little woman
  Her name were Polly Anne,
  John Henry took sick and he had to go to bed,
  Polly Anne drove steel like a man, Lawd, Lawd, etc.

6 Now the Captain told John Henry,
  'I b'lieve my tunnel's sinkin' in'.
  'Stand back, Captain, and doncha be afraid,
  That's nothin' but my hammer catchin' wind, Lawd, Lawd,' etc.

[contd

They say that John Henry was the champion steel driver in the Big Bend Tunnel on the C & O Railroad in West Virginia. The steel drivers' job was to hammer in the long steel bits that made holes for the blasting charges in the tunnel face. His helper, the shaker, held the bit steady and twisted it a quarter turn after every blow of the hammer. One day, in the 1870s, the first mechanical steam drill was introduced, and, in order to test its efficiency, they matched the machine against John Henry. It was 'the flesh against the steam'. John Henry won the contest, but, according to legend at least, died from overstrain. His ballad, built upon a fragment of the Scots ballad, *Lass of Roch Royal*, has grown into epic proportions, and has made itself at home in the whole country.

7 John Henry he told his shaker,
  'Now shaker, why don't you sing?
  I'm throwin' nine pounds from my hips on down,
  Just listen to the cold steel ring, Lawd, Lawd,' *etc.*

8 John Henry he told his shaker,
  'Now shaker, why don't you pray?
  For if I miss this six-foot steel
  Tomorrow'll be your buryin' day, Lawd, Lawd,' *etc.*

9 John Henry he told his Cap'n,
  'Looky yonder, boy, what do I see?
  Your drill's done broke and your hole's done choke,
  And you can't drive steel like me, Lawd, Lawd,' *etc.*

10 John Henry hammerin' in the mountain
  Till the handle of his hammer caught on fire,
  He drove so hard till he broke his po' heart,
  Then he lied down his hammer and he died, Lawd, Lawd, *etc.*

11 Women in the west heard of John Henry's death
  They couldn' hardly stay in bed,
  Stood in the rain, flagged that east-bound train
  'Goin' where that man fell dead, Lawd, Lawd,' *etc.*

12 They took John Henry to the tunnel,
  And they buried him in the sand,
  An' every locomotive come rollin' by
  Say, 'There lays a steel-drivin' man, Lawd, Lawd,' *etc.*

13 Now some say he come from England,
  And some say he come from Spain,
  But I say he's nothin' but a Lou'siana man,
  Leader of a steel-drivin' gang, Lawd, Lawd, *etc.*

66. PICK A BALE O' COTTON

1 Jump down, turn around,
   Pick a bale o' cotton,
   Jump down, turn around,
   Pick a bale a day.
   O — Lawdy, Pick a bale o' cotton,
   O — Lawdy, Pick a bale a day.

2 Ol' Massa gimme one dram to
   Pick a bale o' cotton,
   Ol' Massa gimme one dram to
   Pick a bale a day. *(Chorus)*

3 Me an' my pardner can
   Pick a bale o' cotton, *etc. (Chorus)*

4 I had a little woman could
   Pick a bale o' cotton, *etc. (Chorus)*

5 I b'lieve to my soul I'll
   Pick a bale o' cotton, *etc. (Chorus)*

6 Pick-a, pick-a, pick-a, pick-a,
   Pick-a bale o' cotton, *etc. (Chorus)*

We found this slavery-time cotton-picking song on the Negro prison farms of Texas and Louisiana in the 1930s. Its rapid dance tempo stimulates, but cannot match the swift darting movements of the picker's hands as they move among the dry bolls. No one has ever hand-picked a bale (1500 lb.) of cotton in a day; the best worker can 'snatch' no more than five or six hundred pounds between sunup and sundown. In practice, the leader and chorus sing alternate lines, or the leader sings the first line solo, and then leads the chorus through the rest of the quatrain.

90

67. STEWBALL

Leader	Gang
1 Way out in	Unh-hunh!
Californy	Unh-hunh!
Where old Stewball	Unh-hunh!
Was born,	Was born!
All the jockeys	Unh-hunh!
In the country	Unh-hunh!
Said he blew there	Unh-hunh!
In a storm.	In a storm!

Well, bet on the races,
And you might win, win, win,
Just you bet on the races,
And you might win.

(The remaining stanzas are formed by the leader and the gang in the same manner as the first.)

2 Well, his bridle
Was silver
And his saddle
Was gold
And the price on
His blanket
Hasn't never
Been told. *(Chorus)*

3 Old Mistis
Bet millions
And old Masta
Bet pounds
That old Stewball
Could beat old Molly
On the first
First runnin' round. *(Chorus)*

4 When that big bell
Was tapped on
For the races
To be run,
Old Stewball
He come tremblin'
Like a crim'nal
To be hung. *(Chorus)*

5 'Old Mistis
An' old Masta,
I'm a-riskin'
My life
Just to win a
Great fortune
Just for you and
Your po' little wife.' *(Chorus)*

6 Then that little bell
Was tapped on
And the word was
Given 'Go',
And old Stewball
He shot off
Like an arrow
From a bow. *(Chorus)*

7 Old Molly
Was a-runnin'
Like an express
Passenger train;
But old Stewball
Was a movin'
Like a midnight
Shower of rain. *(Chorus)*

8 The old folks,
They hollered
And the young folks,
They bawled;
But the chillun just said
'Look-a-look-a-look
At the noble
Stewball.' *(Chorus)*

9 The races,
They ended
And the people
Clapped they hands;
And old Stewball
Beat old Molly
Back to the
Grandstand. *(Chorus)*

10 That peafowl
Done holler,
And the turtle dove,
She just moan,
I'm a po' boy
In trouble
And a long ways
From home. *(Chorus)*

A dullish Anglo-Irish come-all-ye ballad recounts the feats of a piebald horse that not only outran everything on four legs, but conversed with his jockey on the progress of the race. Fragments of this ballad remain in currency among white singers, but it was among Negro labourers of Mississippi that it came into its own. *Old Stewball* was their favourite axe song, setting the rhythm and stirring their imaginations, as they sang all together and let their axes fall in unison, hewing their way through the dense forests of the Mississippi Delta. We discovered it in the Mississippi Penitentiary in 1933, in vigorous use as a work song.

68. THE HAMMER SONG

1 Take this hammo,* carry it to the captain,
  Take this hammo, carry it to the captain,
  Take this hammo, carry it to the captain,
  Tell him I'm gone, tell him I'm gone.

2 If he ask you was I runnin', *(three times)*
  Tell him Ize flyin', tell him Ize flyin'.

3 If he asks you was I laughin', *(three times)*
  Tell him Ize cryin', tell him Ize cryin'.

4 I don't want no peas, cornbread or tomatoes, *(three times)*
  They hurts my pride, they hurts my pride.

5 I'm gonna bust right, bust right past that shooter,† *(three times)*
  I'm goin' home, I'm goin' home.

*Hammer.

†Guard.

This powerful, slow-moving song of gang labour, good for men swinging axes, picks, or sledge hammers on various kinds of jobs, occurs in many forms in Virginia, the Carolinas, and Georgia. Indeed, its cadences are commonplace in American Negro folksong. This version, which we recorded in the Virginia State penitentiary, is the fantasy of a Negro convict brooding about an escape attempt from the 'burning hell' of the prison farm.

69. GODAMIGHTY DRAG

Guitarists play in A minor, chords in brackets.

1 Mama and papa,
  Wo-ho, Lawdy,
  Mama and papa,
  Godamighty knows,
  Done tol' me a lie, suh,
  Wo, Lawdy,
  Done tol' me a lie, suh,
  Wo-ho, my Lawd.

2 Done told me they'd pardon me, *etc.*
  Well, next July, suh.

3 June, July and August, *etc.*
  Done come and gone, suh. *etc.*

4 Left me here rollin', *etc.*
  On this ol' farm, suh. *etc.*

5 When Hannah* go to beamin', *etc.*
  Make you think about your mamma. *etc.*

6 When the boys go to steamin', *etc.*
  Make yuh run away, suh. *etc.*

7 O me an' my pardner, *etc.*
  We went to the Brazis. *etc.*

8 And he could not swim, suh, *etc.*
  And he could not swim. *etc.*

9 I crossed him over, *etc.*
  On a live-oak limb. *etc.*

10 Ride, old dog man, *etc.*
   You better ride, old dog man. *etc.*

11 When the Brazis was risin', *etc.*
   Riley walked the water. *etc.*

*The Sun.

A team of eight sturdy Negro axemen recorded this gang work song for us in the Texas penitentiary in 1934. It tells of the despair that leads a convict to attempt an escape under the shotguns of the guards, of his race against the bloodhounds to the swift and dangerous Brazos river and of the legendary Riley, a convict who crossed the river when it was in flood and was thus said to have 'walked the water like Jesus'. (Collected, adapted, and arranged by John and Alan Lomax.)

70. RAILROAD MAN

1 CHORUS 1: *Railroad man ain't got no home, (three times)*
 Here today, Lawd, tomorrow he'll be gone.

2 Well, she took me, took me to her parlour,
 And she cooled me, cooled me with her fan,
 And she swore, swore by the Man that made her,
 'Mother, I do love a railroad man.' *(Chorus 1)*

3 Yes, she told me, told me that she loved me,
 Just to give my, give my poor heart ease,
 Just as soon as, soon as I got in trouble,
 Well, she turned her, turned her back on me. *(Chorus 1)*

4 On a Monday, Monday I was arrested,
 On a Tuesday, was locked up in jail,
 On a Wednesday, my trial was attested,
 On a Thursday, nobody wouldn't go my bail.

CHORUS 2: *Lawd, I was all – already gone, (three times)*
 Nothin' but to bring them yellow women over here.

5 Take these stripes, stripes from around my shoulders,
 Take these chains, chains from around my legs,
 Say, these stripes, stripes they sho' don't worry me,
 But these chains, chains gonna kill me dead. *(Chorus 2)*

In the 1930s when we recorded this song in the Birmingham, Alabama, County Prison, convicts were still worked in chains, on the roads, and in the fields of some localities. This, then, is an authentic chain-gang song, not sad, however, but ironic, nostalgic, and sensual, the proper song to keep a man's heart up while he serves his time. It goes well with jazzy guitar and in simple three-part harmony.

71. FOLLOW THE DRINKIN'-GOURD

1 When the sun comes back and the first quail call,
  Follow the drinkin'-gourd,
  The old man is a-waitin' to carry you to freedom,
  Follow the drinkin'-gourd.

2 Now the river bank will make a mighty good road,
   The dead trees will show you the way,
   Left foot, peg foot, travelin' on,
   Just you follow the drinkin'-gourd.
       Follow the drinkin'-gourd,
       Follow the drinkin'-gourd,
       For the old man is a-waitin' to carry you to freedom,
       Follow the drinkin'-gourd.

3 Where the little river meets the great big one,
   Follow the drinkin'-gourd,
   The old man is a-waitin' to carry you to freedom,
   Follow the drinkin'-gourd.   *(Chorus)*

4 The river ends between two hills,
   Follow the drinkin'-gourd,
   There's another river on the other side,
   Follow the drinkin'-gourd.

In the years before the Civil War, an abolitionist sailor named Peg Leg Joe tramped through Southern Alabama, secretly urging the slaves to run away from their masters. Everywhere he taught the Negroes this song, which not only gave them hope, but provided them with secret directions for the route they should follow: Start in the spring, he sang, with the Dipper as your guide, and, following the peg-toed sign I will leave on the dead trees along the river bank, you will come to the headwaters of the Tombigbee River. Cross the divide to the Ohio River and it will lead you into the free states.

V

Western Songs

LONG before the covered wagons rolled along the Oregon and California trails, the bravest and most fantastic breed of western pioneers had already disappeared. These were the beaver trappers, the so-called mountain men, who, by trading with the Indians, and, frequently, marrying into the tribes, managed to trap millions of dollars' worth of beaver throughout the mountains of the Great Western Divide. We have only one of their songs (*The Wild Mizzourye*, No. 8) and one contemporary account which describes the yearly spree of the mountain men in St Louis. A great hairy hunter lies on his back on the barroom floor and howls out a wild, Indian chant, beating on his rock-hard belly with huge fists, shaking the mirrors with his rhythm.

Of the ways in which ballads eased the painful lives of the forty-niners we have more explicit accounts. Rhymesters rode with the big covered wagon trains, and when the night was fine and the Indians were far away, they unlimbered their banjos and uncorked rhymes about the day's events. In California an anonymous folksong collector gathered these ditties into a tiny book called *Old Put's Golden Songster*, with which his troupe, the Sierra Nevada Rangers, delighted miners' audiences all over California. The Rangers carried derringers as well as banjos, for, although the touchy and temperamental miners often showed their enthusiasm by throwing gold nuggets on the stage, they as frequently accompanied their boos with pistol shots.

The first cowboys were Texans who, for reasons we do not yet understand, found most of their ballad models in northern states. The cattle business had its beginnings in the southern part of Texas that lies along the Gulf Coast, an ideal breeding ground for wild cattle which the patriotic, quick-shooting Anglos from Tennessee preempted from the Mexican ranchers. From the Mexican *vaquero* they acquired their tools and their costume – the *sombrero*, the chaps (*chaparajos*), the *reata*, the Mexican high-cantle saddle, etc. – and from him they learned the art of handling cattle, which included calling to the cattle and singing to them.

Before the Civil War, Texas cattle were slaughtered for their hides and the hides shipped out on coastal barques to the East; but the longhorns had multiplied so rapidly in South Texas during the Civil War, that the ranchers began looking for ways to move their portable wealth north to the middle-western railheads. The first trail herds tried a direct route through the Ozarks to St Louis, but they were bushwhacked by outlaws, the cowboys murdered, and the cattle driven into the hills. Then an enterprising promoter named Colonel Dodge persuaded the Missouri Pacific R.R. to run a spur out into the Kansas plains, and, when this news filtered down into South Texas, big trail herds of longhorns were started north to meet the railroad.

Fighting Indians, fording wild rivers, recovering their cattle after stampedes caused by the sudden storms of the plains, riding day after day through a mile-high cloud of dust across virtually unknown country, the Texas trail bosses pushed their herds north across the plains to Kansas. The Old Chisholm Trail they blazed soon ran all the way to Montana, and the great plains country – formerly the absolute domain of the mounted Plains Indians – quickly filled up with ranches. The trail period lasted no more than twenty years, between 1870 and 1890, but this was sufficient time for the untrammelled genius of the westerners to improvise a culture suitable to themselves – with a dialect, folk legends, customs, handicrafts, and, of course, songs.

The cowboys yelled and sang at their cattle to keep them moving; they crooned to them at night to keep them quiet. There are stories of cowboys who played the fiddle on night guard and of musically inclined longhorns who ambled after them through the dark so as not to miss a note. Round the campfire the cowpunchers chanted to ballads, each cowboy rising in turn to sing 'like a pack of coyotes howling after one another'. Sometimes champion singers met and tried to sing each other down, while the listening cowpokes beat time with their heels in the prairie sod. Naturally, singing went on when whiskey gurgled out of tall bottles at the end of long, throat-parching trails.

Most of these cowboy songs were remakes of the favourites of the fo'c'sle and the bunk-house, but the lonely beauty of the plains, the rhythmic lope of the cowpony, and the mature lyricism of the Southern folk imagination touched these Western variants with magic. Among all the American come-all-ye's, they seem most likely to endure. One example of the three stages of transformation that produced the western ballad is the fo'c'sle song about a pretty Scots girl who longed to leave the hills of Caledon-i-a. The lumberjacks reworked this ballad into three different songs about the hardships of their lives in Canada, in Pennsylvania, and in Michigan. One verse of the Michigan ballad runs,

Our hearts were made of iron, our souls were cased with steel,
The hardships of that winter could never make us yield,
Our food, the dogs would snarl at it, our beds were in the snow,
We suffered worse than murderers up in Michigan-i-o.

The buffalo hunters sang as follows,

Our hearts were cased in buffalo hocks, our souls were cased in steel,
The hardships of that summer were sure to make us reel,
In skinning them damned old stinkers, our lives they had no show,
For the Indians waited to pick us off on the range of the buffalo.

72. THE SIOUX INDIANS

1 I'll sing you a song and it'll be a sad one,
   Of trials and troubles and how first begun,
   We left our dear kindred, our friends and our home,
   Across the wild deserts and mountains to roam. *(twice)*

2 We crossed the Missouri and joined a large train,
   Which bore us o'er mountains and valleys and plains,
   And often of an evening out hunting we'd go
   To shoot the fleet antelope and the wild buffalo. *(twice)*

3 We heard of Sioux Indians all out on the plains,
   A-killing poor drivers and burning their trains,
   A-killing poor drivers with arrows and bows,
   When captured by Indians, no mercy they'd show. *(twice)*

4 We travelled three weeks till we came to the Platte,
   We set up our camp at the head of the flat,
   We spread down our blankets on the green, grassy ground,
   While our mules and our horses were grazing around. *(twice)*

5 While taking refreshment we heard a low yell,
   The whoop of Sioux Indians coming out of the dell,
   We sprang to our rifles with a flash in each eye,
   'Boys,' said our brave leader, 'we'll fight till we die.' *(twice)*

6 They made a bold dash and come near to our train,
   The arrows fell round us like showers of rain,
   But with our long rifles we fed them hot lead,
   Till many a brave warrior around us lay dead. *(twice)*

7 In our little band there were just twenty-four,
   And of the Sioux Indians, five hundred or more,
   We fought them with courage, we said not a word,
   The whoop of the Indians was all could be heard. *(twice)*

8 We shot their bold chief at the head of his band.
   He died like a warrior with his bow in his hand,
   When they saw their brave chief lying dead in his gore,
   They whooped and they yelled and we saw them no more. *(twice)*

9 We travelled by day, guarded camp in the night,
   Till Oregon's mountains look'd high in their might,
   Now in a green valley, beside a clear stream,
   Our journey has ended in the land of our dream. *(twice)*

We recorded this story of a mid-nineteenth-century battle between the Sioux Indians and a Mormon immigrant train from the singing of an ex-cowboy in Austin, Texas, in 1935.

73. SWEET BETSY FROM PIKE

Brisk, with a strong swing ♩ = 126

1. Did you e - ver hear tell of sweet Bet - sy from Pike, Who cross'd the wide prair - ies with her lo - ver, Ike? With two yoke of cat - tle and one spot - ted hog, A — tall Shang - hai roost - er and an old yal - ler dog.

CHORUS
Sing too-ra - li - oo-ra-li - oo-ra - li - aye, Sing too-ra - li - oo-ra-li - oo-ra - li - aye.

1 Did you ever hear tell of sweet Betsy from Pike,
Who cross'd the wide prairies with her lover, Ike?
With two yoke of cattle and one spotted hog,
A tall Shanghai rooster and an old yaller dog.
Sing too-ra-li-oo-ra-li-oo-ra-li-aye,
Sing too-ra-li-oo-ra-li-oo-ra-li-aye.

2 They swam the wild rivers and climbed the tall peaks,
And camped on the prairies for weeks upon weeks,
Starvation and cholera, hard work and slaughter,
They reached Californy, spite of hell and high water. *(Chorus)*

3 They soon reached the desert where Betsy gave out,
And down in the sand she lay rolling about,
While Ike in great wonder looked on in surprise,
Sayin', 'Get up now, Betsy, you'll get sand in your eyes.' *(Chorus)*

4 The Indians come down in a wild yelling horde,
And Betsy got skeered they would scalp her adored,
So behind the front wagon wheel Betsy did crawl,
And fought off the Indians with musket and ball. *(Chorus)*

5 They stopped off at Salt Lake to inquire the way,
And Brigham declared that sweet Betsy should stay,
But Betsy got frightened and ran like a deer,
While Brigham stood pawing the ground like a steer. *(Chorus)*

6 One morning they climbed up a very high hill,
And with wonder looked down upon old Placerville,
Ike shouted and said as he cast his eyes down,
'Sweet Betsy, my darlin', we've got to Hangtown.' *(Chorus)*

7 Long Ike and Sweet Betsy attended a dance,
Where Ike wore a pair of his Pike County pants,
And Betsy was covered with ribbon and rings,
Quoth Ike, 'You're an angel, but where are your wings?' *(Chorus)*

8 A miner said, 'Betsy, will you dance with me?'
'I will that, Old Hoss, if you don't make too free,
But don't dance me hard, do you want to know why?
Doggone ye, I'm chock full of strong alkali!'

9 Long Ike and sweet Betsy got married, of course,
But Ike, getting jealous, obtained a divorce,
While Betsy, well satisfied, said with a shout,
'Goodbye, you big lummox, I'm glad you backed out.'

Perhaps the best of all the songs set to the tune that Englishmen know as *Villikins and his Dinah*, this gold-rush ballad tells the rollicking story of a covered wagon trek to California in the days of forty-nine. Such songs were performed by the professional entertainers who toured the gold camps, and were circulated in the little pocket song books of that day.

74. THE OX-DRIVING SONG

1 On the fourteenth day of October-o
I hitched my team in order-o,
To drive the hills of Salud-i-o,
To my rol, to my rol, to my ride-i-o,
To my rol, to my rol, to my ride-i-o,
*To my rol, to my rol, to my **ride-i-o,***
To my ride-i-o, ride-i-o,
To my rol, to my rol, to my ride-i-o.

2 When I got there the hills were steep,
'Twould make a tender hearted person weep,
To hear me cuss and pop my whip,
To see my oxen pull and slip. *(Chorus)*

3 I pop my whip, I bring the blood,
I make my leaders take the mud,
I grab the wheels and turn them round,
With a long, long pull we're on hard ground. *(Chorus)*

4 When I get home I'll have revenge,
I'll leave my family among my friends,
I'll bid adieu to the whip and line,
And drive no more in the winter time. *(Chorus)*

Even cowboys and muleskinners acknowledged that the ox driver had a precision, virulence, and ingenuity in his profanity that no one could match. His animals literally wouldn't pull unless he lashed at them with a tremendous string of oaths. This violent song, which John Lomax collected from Herman Weaver in the Texas pine woods, comes out of the tough bandit-ridden Missouri Hills of the 1860s.

75. JESSE JAMES

1 Jesse James was a lad that killed many a man,
  And robbed that Danville train,
  But that dirty little coward that shot Mister Howard,
  Has laid poor Jesse in his grave.
    Poor Jesse had a wife to mourn all her life,
    His children, they were brave,
    Robert Ford caught his eye and shot him on the sly,
    And they laid poor Jesse in his grave.

2 It was his brother Frank stuck up the Pittsfield Bank,
  And carried the money from the town,
  It was in this very place that they had a little race,
  For they shot Captain Sheets to the ground. *(Chorus)*

3 They went to the crossing not very far from there,
  And there they did the same,
  With the agent on his knees, he delivered up the keys,
  To the outlaws, Frank and Jesse James. *(Chorus)*

4 It was on a Wednesday night, the moon was shining bright,
  They stopped the Glendale train,
  He robbed from the rich and he gave to the poor,
  He'd a heart, and a hand and a brain. *(Chorus)*

5 It was on a Saturday night when Jesse was at home,
  Talking with his family brave,
  Robert Ford's pistol ball brought him tumbling from the wall
  And they laid poor Jesse in his grave. *(Chorus)*

6 It was Robert Ford, that dirty little coward,
  I wonder how he does feel,
  For he ate of Jesse's bread, and he slept in Jesse's bed,
  And then laid poor Jesse in his grave. *(Chorus)*

7 This song was made by Billy Gashade
  As soon as the news did arrive,
  He said there was no man with the law in his hand,
  Could take Jesse James when alive. *(Chorus)*

America's Robin Hood was a Rebel soldier, who returned to his home state, Missouri, after the Civil War and, finding some hard and unjust usage at the hands of his Union neighbours, became a train robber and bank-buster. He ranged over the whole Middlewest with his band, striking quickly, moving fast and far and striking again, until the name Jesse James became a legend throughout the land. In 1882, while he was living quietly with his family under the alias of Howard, he was shot from behind by one of his own gang, Robert Ford, for the sake of the $10,000 reward. His ballad, written by an anonymous people's poet, is known in every stage of the Union. John A. Lomax discovered it in the early 1900s.

76. RYE WHISKEY

1 If the ocean was whiskey, and I was a duck,
  I'd dive to the bottom and never come up.
  Rye whiskey, rye whiskey,
  Rye whiskey I cry,
  If you don't give me rye whiskey
  I surely will die.
  E . . . ah . . . h . . . (hiccup) (hiccup) . . Ah.

2 But the ocean ain't whiskey, and I ain't no duck,
  So let's round up the cattle and then we'll get drunk. *(Chorus)*

3 But if I get boozy, my money's my own,
  And them that don't like me can leave me alone. *(Chorus)*

4 I'll ramble, I'll tramble this wide world alone,
  I'm just a rabble* soldier and Dixie's my home. *(Chorus)*

5 O Mollie, O Mollie, I've told you before,
  Just make me a pallet and we'll lie on the floor. *(Chorus)*

6 Jack o' Diamonds, Jack o' Diamonds,† I know you of old,
  You've robbed my poor pockets of silver and gold. *(Chorus)*

7 O whiskey you villain, you've been my downfall,
  You've kicked me, you've cuffed me, but I love you for all. *(Chorus)*

8 O whiskey, O whiskey, you're no friend to me,
  You killed my old daddy, goldarn you, try me. *(Chorus)*

9 Beefsteak when I'm hungry, whiskey when I'm dry,
  Greenbacks‡ when I'm hard-up, sweet heaven when I die. *(Chorus)*

10 For work I'm too lazy and beggin's too slow,
   Train robbin's too dangerous, to gamblin' I'll go. *(Chorus)*

11 I'll buy my own whiskey, I'll make my own stew,
   If I get drunk, Madam, it's nothin' to you. *(Chorus)*

12 O Mollie, O Mollie, I've told you before,
   Your parents don't like me because I'm so poor. *(Chorus)*

13 I'll tune up my fiddle, and rosin my bow,
   And make myself welcome wherever I go. *(Chorus)*

14 I'll eat when I'm hungry and drink when I'm dry,
   If the hard times don't kill me, I'll live till I die. *(Chorus)*

15 Way up in the mountains, I wander alone,
   I'm drunk as the Devil, so leave me alone. *(Chorus)*

*Southern soldier in the Civil War.
†Cowboy card game.
‡Dollars.

After the Civil War there was a mass migration of homeless and impoverished Southern soldiers to Texas and farther West. These wild buckaroos became buffalo hunters, Indian fighters, bad men, and cowboys, and this is their hymn of praise to the only friend who was certain to give them a warm greeting at the end of a long, dusty trail. The roots of the song are the same as those of *On Top of Old Smokey* and the English *Wagoner Lad.* John A. Lomax took down numerous versions of this drinking song from cowboys in the early 1900s.

77. THE RANGE OF THE BUFFALO

Moderately slow ♩.= 66

1. It hap-pened in Jacks-bo-ro, boys, in the year of seven-ty-three, A man by the name of Cre-go ___ came step-ping up to me, Says,'How do you do, young fel-low, ___ and how would you like to go ___ And spend one sum-mer sea-son on the range of the buf-fa-lo?'

1 It happened in Jacksboro, boys, in the year of seventy-three,
A man by the name of Crego came stepping up to me,
Says, 'How do you do, young fellow, and how would you like to go . . .
And spend one summer season on the range of the buffalo?'

2 It's me bein' out of employment, boys, to Crego I did say,
'This goin' out on the buffalo range depends upon the pay.
But if you will pay good wages, give transportation, too,
I think, sir, I will go with you and stay the summer through.'

3 It's now we've crossed Pease River, boys, our troubles just begun,
The first damned tail I went to rip, Christ, how I cut my thumb,
While skinning the damned old stinkers our lives they had no show,
For the Indians waited to pick us off on the range of the buffalo.

4 Our hearts were cased in buffalo hocks, our souls were cased in steel,
The hardship of that summer would nearly make us reel,
The water was salty as hell fire, the beef I could not go,
And the Indians waited to pick us off on the range of the buffalo.

5 The season being over, boys, old Crego he did say,
That we had been extravagant, were in debt to him that day,
We coaxed him and we begged him, but still it was no go,
So we left his damned old bones to bleach on the range of the buffalo.

6 It's now we've crossed Pease River, boys, and homeward we are bound,
No more in that hellfired country will ever we be found,
Go back to our wives and sweethearts, tell others not to go,
For God's forsaken the buffalo range, and the damned old buffalo.

This has been called the finest single American ballad. It recounts one episode in the most horrible mass slaughter of game in all history. The federal government, in order to destroy the food supply of the untamed and undefeated Plains Indians, put a bounty on buffalo hides. Trainloads of hunters swarmed into the plains and shot the buffalo by the tens of thousands. It was said that in one place a man could walk for a mile on buffalo bones and never put his foot to earth. In a few years the buffalo had disappeared. The Plains Indians were defeated and only this memory of the tough, universally despised buffalo hunter remained. The ballad, in a come-all-ye style, is a derivative of a lumberjack song, and both are set to a ballad air common in Scotland. A discovery of John A. Lomax in the early 1900s.

78. THE OLD CHISHOLM TRAIL

Moderately slow jog-trot ♩ = 84

1. Come a-long, boys, and lis-ten to my tale, I'll tell you of my trou-bles on the Old Chis-holm Trail. Come-a-ki-yi-yip-py, come-a-ki-yi-yea, Come-a-ki-yi-yip-py,come-a-ki-yi-yea. 2. A etc. ki-yi-yea.

1 Come along, boys, and listen to my tale,
  I'll tell you of my troubles on the Old Chisholm Trail.
  Come-a-ki-yi-yippy, come-a-ki-yi-yea, (twice)

2 A ten-dollar horse and a forty-dollar saddle,
  And I'm goin' punchin' Texas cattle. *(Chorus)*

3 It's bacon and beans most every day,
  I'd sooner be eatin' prairie hay. *(Chorus)*

4 Woke up one mornin' on the Old Chisholm Trail,
  My rope in my hand and a heifer by the tail. *(Chorus)*

5 Stray in the herd and the boss said kill it,
  So we bedded that stray in the bottom of the skillet. *(Chorus)*

6 It's rainin' and hailin' and blowin' mighty cold,
  An' these longhorn sonsaguns are gettin' hard to hold. *(Chorus)*

7 I jumped in my saddle and I gave a little yell,
  The tail cattle broke and the leaders went to hell. *(Chorus)*

8 My feet in the stirrups, my seat in the sky,
  Gonna quit herdin' cows in the sweet bye and bye. *(Chorus)*

9 I don't give a damn if they never do stop,
  I'll ride as long as an eight-day clock. *(Chorus)*

10 So I herded and I hollered and done very well,
  Till the boss said, 'Bill, just let um go to hell.' *(Chorus)*

11 Now my old boss is a mighty fine man,
  You know there's whiskey wherever he lands. *(Chorus)*

12 We rounded um up and put um on the cars,
  And that was the last of the old Two Bars.*

13 I went to my boss to draw my roll,
  He had me figured out five dollars in the hole. *(Chorus)*

14 Me and my boss we had a little chat,
  And I slammed him in the face with my ten gallon hat. *(Chorus)*

15 I'm goin' to town to spend my money,
  Then I'm goin' back South to see my honey. *(Chorus)*

*The herd brand.

The Chisholm Trail ran for a thousand miles from San Antonio into Montana and Wyoming, and there is said to be a stanza of this cow-punching song for every mile of the way. The refrain may have been derived from one of the old French *voyageur* paddling songs; the verses, composed *ad lib* around the camp fire or on horseback by many singers, give a realistic picture of life on the cattle trail in the 1870s and 1880s. Scores of versions of this cowboy epic were recorded by John A. Lomax in the early 1900s.

79. WHOOPIE-TI-YI-YO

Rather slow and melancholy ♩ = 144

1. As I walked out one mornin' for plea-sure, I saw a cow-punch-er come a-ri-din' a-long, His head was throwed back and his spurs _____ was a-jing-lin', As he ap-proach'd me, singin' this song. Whoopie-

CHORUS

-ti-yi-yo, git a-long; _____ lit-tle do-gies, It's your mis-for-tune and none of my own, Whoopie-ti-yi-yo, git a-long, _____ lit-tle do-gies, For you know Wy-om-ing will be your new home.

1 As I walked out one mornin' for pleasure,
   I saw a cow-puncher come a-ridin' along,
   His head was throwed back and his spurs was a-jinglin',
   As he approach'd me, singin' this song.
   CHORUS 1: *Whoopie-ti-yi-yo, git along, little dogies,*
       It's your misfortune and none of my own,
       Whoopie-ti-yi-yo, git along, little dogies,
       For you know Wyoming will be your new home.

2 It's early in the springtime we round up them dogies,
   Mark um and brand um and bob off their tails,
   Drive up the hosses, load up the chuckwagon,
   And throw them little dogies out on the trail.
   CHORUS 2: *Whoopie-ti-yi-yo, git along, little dogies,*
       You know Wyoming will be your new home,
       It's whoopin' and yellin' and damnin' them dogies
       To our soul's perdition and none of their own.

3 Now some boys, they goes up the trail for pleasure,
   But that's where they get it most awfully wrong,
   For you ain't got no idea of the trouble they give us,
   As we go drivin' them dogies along. *(Chorus 1)*

4 It's you'll be beef for Uncle Sam's Injuns,
   It's beef, heap-beef I hear them cry,
   Git along, git along, git along, you little dogies,
   You're gwine-a be beef steers bye and bye. *(Chorus 2)*

The curious and ironic history of this western cowboy lullaby is now clear. Seamus Ennis found its earliest variant, *Christ Child Lullaby*, in Western Ireland, where the folk say that Mary sang it to the baby Jesus. Also in Erse there is the satiric lament of the old man left home by his young wife to mind a baby which is 'none of his own'. The modern Anglo-Irish variant of this complaint has much the same tune and refrain as the American cowboy song, and in 1940 I found a Montana version which was half the Irish song and half the cowboy lullaby. No more suitable 'dogie' song could have been chosen, since the little dogie, who lags behind the herd and is the constant charge of the cowboys, is an 'orphan calf whose mammy has died in a boghole, and whose daddy has run off with another cow'. The cowboy has become the crooning foster-parent, 'rocking a baby that's none of his own'. This song was discovered in Fort Worth, Texas, in the early 1900s by John A. Lomax.

80. THE DYING COWBOY

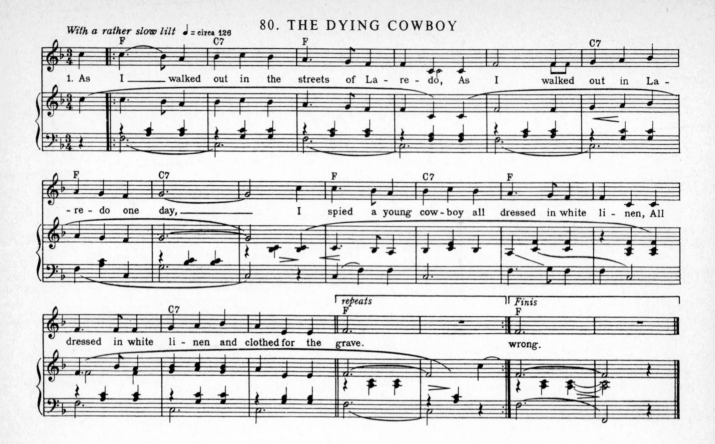

With a rather slow lilt ♩ = circa 126

1. As I _____ walked out in the streets of La - re - do, As I walked out in La - re - do one day, _____ I spied a young cow - boy all dressed in white li - nen, All dressed in white li - nen and clothed for the grave. *repeats* wrong. *Finis*

1 As I walked out in the streets of Laredo,
   As I walked out in Laredo one day,
   I spied a young cowboy all dressed in white linen,
   All dressed in white linen and clothed for the grave.

2 'Once in my saddle I used to go dashin',
   Once in my saddle I used to look gay,
   I first took to drinkin' and then to card playin',
   Got shot in the breast and I'm dyin' today.

3 'Send six rowdy cowboys to carry me coffin
   Send six pretty ladies to sing me a song,
   Take me to the green valley and lay the sod o'er me,
   For I'm a young cowboy and I know I've done wrong.

4 'So beat your drums slowly and play your fifes lowly,
   And play the dead march as you carry me on,
   Take me to the grave-yard and throw the clods o'er me,
   For I'm a wild cowboy and I know I've done wrong.

5 'Go bring me back a cup of cold water
   To cool these parched lips,' the cowboy then said.
   Before I returned, his soul had departed
   And gone to the round-up . . . this cowboy lay dead.

6 We swung our ropes slowly and rattled our spurs lowly,
   And gave a wild whoop as we carried him along,
   For we all loved our comrade, so brave, young and handsome,
   We all loved our comrade, although he'd done wrong.

This cowboy variant of the British *Unfortunate Rake* was by far the most popular of all folk songs among the cowboys. Set to a come-all-ye tune, it summed up the lonely and brooding thoughts of the man with whom death always rode as a close companion. Numerous versions were recorded by John A. Lomax in the early 1900s.

81. I'M A-RIDIN' OLD PAINT

1 I'm a-ridin' old Paint, a-leadin' old Fan,
  I'm off to Montana for to throw the hoolihan,
  We feed um in the coulees and water in the draw,
  Their tails are all matted and their backs are all raw.
    Ride around the little dogies,
    Ride around them slow,
    For the fiery and the snuffy
    Are rarin' to go.

2 I've worked in the army, and worked on the farm,
  All I've got to show is just this muscle in my arm,
  Blisters on my seat, callous on my hands,
  And I'm off to Montan' for to throw the hoolihan. *(Chorus)*

3 Old Bill Jones had a daughter and a son,
  One went to college and the other went wrong,
  His wife, she died in a pool-room fight,
  But still he keeps singin' from mornin' till night. *(Chorus)*

4 Now when I die, don't bury me at all,
  Just saddle my pony, lead him out of the stall,
  Tie my bones in the saddle, turn our faces to the west
  And we'll ride the prairie that we love best. *(Chorus)*

This quiet song of the Western rider, reflecting the vastness and solitude of the Western plains and the recurrent melancholy of the lonely cowboy, was found by Margaret Larkin and popularized by Carl Sandburg.

82. THE ZEBRA DUN

1 We were camped on the plains at the head of the Cimmaron,
When along come a stranger and stopp'd to arger some,
He looked so very foolish, we began to look around,
We figgered he was a greenhorn, just escaped from town.

2 We asked if he'd had any breakfast, he hadn't had a smear,
So we opened up the chuckbox and bade him have his share,
He took a cup of coffee, some biscuits and some beans,
And then he begin to talk about them foreign kings and queens.

3 Such an educated feller, his thoughts just came in herds,
He astonished all us cowboys with his jawbreakin' words,
He just kept on a-talkin' till he made the boys all sick,
And they began to look around just how to play a trick.

4 He said he'd lost his job down on the 7-D,*
And was goin' cross the plains to strike the Santa Fe,
He didn't say how come it, some trouble with the boss,
But said he'd like to borrow a nice fat saddle hoss.

5 This tickled all the boys to death, they laughed way down in their sleeves,
'We'll lend you a horse, just as fresh and fat as you please.'
Shorty grabbed a lariat and roped old Zebra Dun,
Turned him over to the stranger and waited for the fun.

6 Old Dunny was an outlaw that had growed so awful wild,
He could paw the white out of the moon every jump for a mile;
But Dunny stood right still, as if he didn't know,
Till the stranger had him saddled and ready for to go.

7 When the stranger hit the saddle, old Dunny quit the earth,
And traveled right straight up for all that he was worth,
He was standin' on his head, a-havin' wall-eyed fits,
With his hind feet in the stirrups and his front ones in the bits.

8 You could see the tops of mountains under Dunny every jump,
But the stranger, he was growed there just like a camel's hump,
Yes, the stranger sat upon him and curled his black moustache,
Just like a summer boarder, a-waitin' for his hash.

9 He thumped him in the shoulders and spurred him when he whirled,
To show them flunky punchers that he was the wolf of the world,
And when he had dismounted once more upon the ground,
We knew he was a thoroughbred and not a gent from town.

10 O he could twirl a lariat and he didn't do it slow,
He could catch the forefeet nine out of ten for any kind of dough,
There's one thing and a shore thing I've learned since I've been born
That every educated feller ain't a plum greenhorn.

*A ranch.

The practical joke played on the greenhorn was the theme of countless tales and songs among sailors, lumberjacks, teamsters, miners, and cowboys – all the footloose, freeborn workingmen who opened up the American frontier.

This yarn of the dude who turned the joke back on his persecutors is one of the classics of western anonymous verse. Discovered by John A. Lomax.

83. MY GOVERNMENT CLAIM

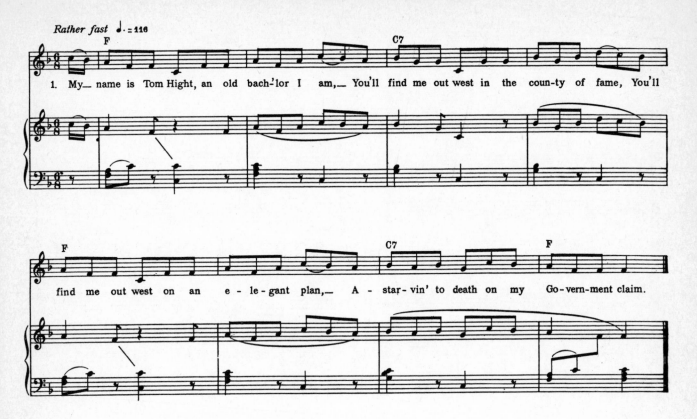

Rather fast ♩. = 116

1. My name is Tom Hight, an old bach'-lor I am,— You'll find me out west in the coun-ty of fame, You'll find me out west on an e-le-gant plan,— A-star-vin' to death on my Go-vern-ment claim.

1 My name is Tom Hight, an old bach'lor I am,
   You'll find me out west in the county of fame,
   You'll find me out west on an elegant plan,
   A-starvin' to death on my Government claim.

2 Hurrah for Greer County, the land of the free,
   The land of the bedbug, grasshopper and flea,
   I'll sing of its praises, I'll tell of its fame,
   While starving to death on my Government claim.

3 My house it is built out of National soil,
   Its walls are erected according to Hoyle,
   Its roof has no pitch, but is level and plain,
   I always get wet if it happens to rain.

4 My clothes are all ragged, my language is rough,
   My bread is corndodgers, both solid and tough,
   But yet I am happy and live at my ease,
   On sorghum molasses, and bacon and cheese.

5 How happy I am when I crawl into bed,
   A rattlesnake hisses a tune at my head,
   A gay little centipede all without fear,
   Crawls over my pillow and into my ear.

6 Now all you claimholders I hope you will stay,
   And chew your hardtack till you're toothless and grey,
   But as for myself I'll no longer remain
   To starve like a dog on my Government claim.

7 Farewell to Greer County, farewell to the West,
   I'll travel back east to the girl I love best,
   I'll travel to Texas and marry me a wife,
   Cry quits on corndodgers the rest of my life.

8 Goodbye to Greer County, where blizzards arise,
   Where the sun never sinks and the flea never dies,
   And the wind never ceases, but always remains,
   Till it starves us all out on our Government claim.

After the Civil War, when huge tracts of Federal land were parcelled out, a man could establish his claim to 160 acres for a small fee, provided he lived on it for five years. As this rollicking ballad shows, five years in an Oklahoman sod shanty was a fair price to pay for a homestead. John A. Lomax found this song in Oklahoma.

84. BLACK JACK DAVY

1 Black Jack Davy come a-ridin' through the woods,
Singing songs so gayly,
Sang so loud he made the wild woods ring,
Charmed the heart of a lady,
Charmed the heart of a wife.

2 Old man come ridin' home that night,
Inquiring for his lady,
The servant spoke before he thought,
'She's gone with the Black Jack Davy,
She's gone with the Black Jack boy.'

3 'Go saddle for me my buckskin horse
With a hundred dollar saddle,
Point out to me their waggon tracks
And after them I'll travel,
After them I'll ride.'

4 Well, he had not rode till the midnight moon,
Till he saw the campfire gleaming,
And he heard the Gipsy's big guitar
And the voice of the lady singing
The song of the gipsy Dave.

5 'Will you forsake your house and home,
Will you forsake your baby,
Will you forsake the one you love,
To roam with the Black Jack Davy,
To roam with the Black Jack boy?'

6 'Yes, I'll forsake my house and home,
Yes, I'll forsake my baby,
And I'll forsake the one I love,
To roam with the Black Jack Davy,
To roam with the Black Jack boy.'

7 'Take off, take off your buckskin gloves,
Made of Spanish leather,
Give to me your lilywhite hand,
And we'll go back home together,
We'll go back home again.'

8 'Yes, I'll take off my buckskin gloves,
Made of Spanish leather,
Give to you my lilywhite hand,
And bid farewell forever,
And bid farewell, goodbye.'

9 'Last night I lay in my own feather bed,
By the side of my little baby,
Tonight I'll lie in the mud and rain,
By the side of the Black Jack Davy,
By the side of the Black Jack boy.'

In America the Scots *Gypsie Laddie* turned into a Western highwayman called **Black Jack Davy**. This version is a composite of Texas and Oklahoma texts, recorded by us for the Library of Congress.

85. THE ROVING GAMBLER

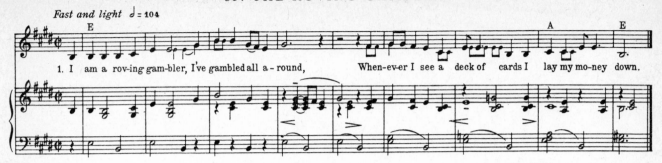

Fast and light ♩ = 104

1. I am a rov-ing gam-bler, I've gambled all a-round, When-ev-er I see a deck of cards I lay my mo-ney down.

1 I am a roving gambler,
   I've gambled all around,
   Whenever I see a deck of cards
   I lay my money down.

2 I had not been in New York Town
   Many more weeks than three,
   Till I fell in love with a pretty little gal,
   And she fell in love with me.

3 She took me in her parlour
   And she cooled me with her fan,
   And she whispered low in her mother's ear,
   'I love that gamblin' man.'

4 'O daughter, O dear daughter
   How can you treat me so,
   To leave your dear old mother,
   And with a gambler go?'

5 'O Mother, O dear Mother,
   You know I love you well,
   But the love I have for the gamblin' man.
   No human tongue can tell.'

6 'I wouldn't marry a farmer,
   For he's always in the rain,
   All I want is the gamblin' man
   Who wears the big gold chain.'

7 'I hear the train a-comin',
   A-comin' round the curve,
   A-whistlin' and a-strainin',
   A-strainin' every nerve.'

8 'O mother, O dear mother,
   I'll tell you if I can,
   If you ever see me comin' back
   It'll be with the gamblin' man.'

A long-time favourite song of hoboes, hard guys, and men of the roads, this is a travel-worn American cousin of the British *Roving Journeyman*. Variants in which the journeyman has become a soldier, a guerrilla fighter, or a gambler have been found throughout the South and southern Middlewest. Recently, the song has been spread through numerous recorded versions.

VI
Modern Times

THE first folk heroes to make a hit with nineteenth-century America were the audacious hunters and flatboatmen from the Ohio River – Davy Crockett and Mike Fink. If there was anything they loved more than fighting, it was *talking* about fighting. Before the redoubtable Mike Fink waded into a victim, he would try to terrify him with his brag,

'I'm a Salt River Roarer! I'm a ring-tailed squealer! I'm a regular screamer from the old Mississipp'. I'm the very infant that refused his milk before his eyes were open, and called for a bottle of old Rye. I love the women and I'm full of fight! I'm half wild horse and half cock-eyed alligator and the rest of me is crooked snags an' red hot snappin' turkle. I can hit like fourth-proof lightnin' an' every lick I make in the woods lets in an acre of sunshine. I can out-run, out-jump, out-shoot, out-brag, out-drink an' out-fight, rough-an'-tumble, no holds barred, any man on both sides of the river from Pittsburgh to New Orleans. Come on you flatters, you milk-white mechanics, an' see how tough I am to chaw! I ain't had a fight for two days and I'm spilin' for exercise. Cock-a-doodle-doo!'

Hardboiled Texas cowboys in their liquor versified their fighting brags,

Raised in a cane brake, suckled by a bear,
The click of a six-shooter is music to my ear!
The further up the creek you go, the worse they get,
And I'm from the head of it! WHOOP-EE!

On the frontier this language was not all wind. Lively play of knotty fists, tomahawks, bowie knives, six-guns, often ensued. The scout who had the most Indian scalps at his belt, the flatboatman who carried eye-balls in his pouch, the lumberjack who had stomped his steel caulks into the faces of most men, the cowboy with the most notches on his gun, the city thug who escaped the law after a machine-gunning – a gallery of 'ornery' characters, who rejoiced in violence for its own sake, have been the objects of hero-worship by some.

Though the myth of the outlaw-killer was, in a measure, the offspring of frontier necessity, its antecedents were European. Indeed, its deepest roots lie in the unconscious of all mankind. At the level of folk tradition, there has always been a public expression of sympathy for the rebel, no matter how violent and destructive. Poverty, sexual deprivation, illness, caste and class lines – all these things, and many more, torment us, and we rejoice inwardly when the bandit or gunman strikes back in blind fury against the society and the conventions we secretly hold responsible for our sorrows.

A great many of the most stirring folk songs and ballads in English, from *Henry Martin* to *Brady and Duncan* (No. 90) tell the stories of criminals and jailbirds. In the ubiquitously popular form, 'the goodnight', the criminal is given an opportunity to tell his story and make an appeal for sympathy as he stands upon the scaffold. In other ballads the stories of crimes are reported with an obvious relish, although an apologetic moral may be hastily tacked on at the end.

The heroes of another school of modern American folksong were railroadmen, hoboes, and the railroad itself. For a people naturally restless, locked in a vast prison of land, the railroad train was much more than a convenient means of transportation. It stood for freedom, opportunity, wealth, romance, adventure, and progress. Americans still love to watch their big trains thunder by, but sixty years ago country boys regarded Casey Jones and his kind as so many Lancelots mounted on magnificent iron horses.

The old time engineer designed his own personal whistle in the shape of a cluster of pipes upon which he could almost play a tune, and the lonesome wail of these whistles in the night called many restless young men to spend their lives hoboing round the country. The great period of the professional tramp, between 1900 and 1935, produced a folk literature all its own.

When a woman blue, she hang her little head an' cry,
When a man get blue, he grab that train an' ride . . .

Negro folk musicians consciously incorporated the moaning of locomotive whistles and the syncopated rhythms of the train into their music. *The Yancey Special*, a boogie-woogie classic known to all jazz lovers, was an attempt by its composer to match the mighty music of the trains that drummed by his Chicago slum flat; and one of the classic Negro blues, *Goin' North*, is a composition in which the guitar imitates every sound of a fast freight headed for Chicago, carrying a Negro hobo to a land where 'he'll be better known'. Anyone who listens carefully can hear railroad themes all through jazz, the blues, and hillbilly music.

The creators of contemporary styles of American folk music have not, as certain scholars expected, ceased to make and sing folk songs in urban, twentieth-century America. Living in city slums, working on huge industrial projects, watching T V, they continue to come forth with fresh song ideas, startling instrumental colours, new rhythms, and original themes, while they hold stubbornly to certain old songs that retain their expressive importance even in a streamlined setting. There are still many mysteries in the great human jungle that is America; there are aesthetic needs that Hollywood and Tin Pan Alley and Television Row do not yet know how to satisfy, and my own prayer and certainty is that there always will be. Tomorrow the Holy Rollers, the hillbillies, the blues shouters, the gospel singers – the Leadbellies, the Guthries, the Armstrongs, the Sister Tharpes – who have formed our twentieth-century folk music, will be replaced by other folk artists. These new singers will give voice to the deep feelings and the unspoken needs of their own time, as have all the folk singers of the past.

86. BIRMINGHAM JAIL

1 Write me a letter,
  Send it by mail,
  Back it in care of
  The Birmingham Jail.
  Birmingham Jail, love,
  Birmingham Jail,
  Back it in care of
  The Birmingham Jail.

2 Bird in a cage, love,
  Bird in a cage,
  Dying for freedom,
  Ever a slave, *etc.*

3 Build me a castle
  On the mountain so high,
  So I can see her
  As she passes by, *etc.*

4 If you don't love me,
  Love who you please,
  Throw your arms round me,
  Give my heart ease, *etc.*

5 Down in the valley,
  Valley so low,
  Late in the evening
  Hear the train blow, *etc.*

Hillbilly singers crooned *Birmingham Jail* into popularity in the 1920s, but it appears to have originated among Negro prisoners in the Deep South at an earlier date. Like so many Southern songs, this one has probably crossed the Jim Crow line a number of times, and may cross it again.

87. JOHN HARTY

1. John Har-ty was a des-perate lit-tle man, Car-ried a gun ev-'ry day, Killed a man in the West Vir-gi-nia land, Ought-a seen lit-tle John-ny get a-way, Ought-a seen lit-tle John-ny get a-way.

1 John Harty was a desperate little man,
  Carried a gun ev'ry day,
  Killed a man in the West Virginia land,
  Oughta seen little Johnny get away. *(twice)*

2 John Harty was standin' at the bar-room door,
  He had no hand in the game,
  Up stepped his little woman and threw a quarter down,
  Says, 'Count John Harty in the game.' *(twice)*

3 John Harty lost his last fifty cents,
  Was all he had in the game,
  He drew out his 44 gun
  And blowed out that poor boy's brains. *(twice)*

4 John Harty had ten miles for to go
  And half of that he run,
  He run till he came to the broad river bank,
  And he fell to his breast and he swum. *(twice)*

5 John Harty went to the tunnel, poor boy,
  Thought he would make his getaway,
  Up stepped the sheriff and took him by the arm,
  Said, 'Johnny, come and go with me.' *(twice)*

6 John Harty's father come for him,
  He come for to go his bail,
  No bail was allowed for a murderin' man,
  And they shoved John Harty back in jail. *(twice)*

7 They took John Harty to his hangin' ground,
  They hung him there to die,
  The very last words that poor boy said,
  'My forty gun never told a lie.' *(twice)*

8 'I've been to the East and I been to the West,
  'I've travelled this wide world around,
  I've been to the river and I been baptized,
  Now I'm on my hanging ground.' *(twice)*

9 John Harty had one pretty little woman,
  Dress she wore was blue,
  She gave a long and lonesome cry,
  And I wish my wife was true. *(twice)*

10 John Harty had another little woman,
  The dress she wore was red,
  She gave one long and lonesome cry,
  And I wish my wife was dead. *(twice)*

John Harty, a West Virginia Negro tunnel-worker, killed a man in a gambling dispute, and was hanged on 19 January 1894. At the scaffold he is said to have advised all young men to take warning by him and avoid card-playing and whiskey-drinking. This ballad so closely resembles *John Henry* that the two songs are often confused; but, in text and tune, *John Harty* is clearly of mountain white origin. Indeed, until recently, it was not known outside of the Southern Appalachians where it is a favourite banjo and guitar piece. (Adapted and arranged by A. Lomax.)

88. POOR BOY

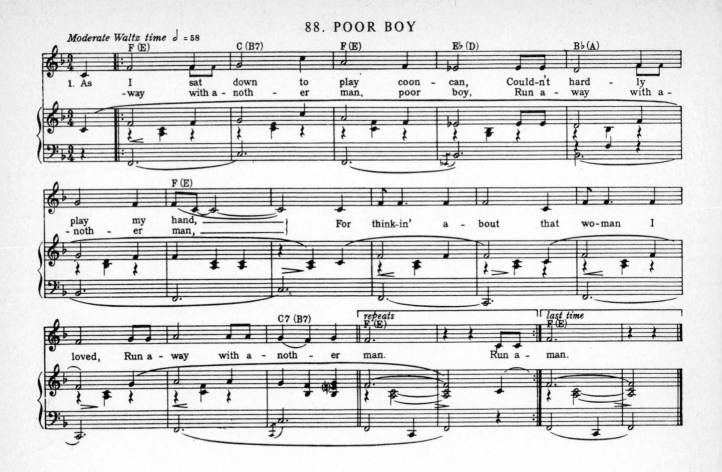

Moderate Waltz time ♩ = 58

1 As I sat down to play coon-can,
  Couldn't hardly play my hand,
  For thinkin' about that woman I loved,
  Run away with another man,
     Run away with another man, poor boy,
     Run away with another man,
     For thinkin' about that woman I loved,
     Run away with another man.

3 I swung onto a passing car
  And I walked back up the aisle,
  I pulled out my big forty-some-odd*
  And I shot that brownskin child,
     And I shot that brownskin child, poor boy, *etc.*

5 My mammy's in the cold, cold ground,
  My daddy's gone away,
  My sister's married a gambling man
  And I have gone astray,
     And I have gone astray, poor boy, *etc.*

.2 I went down to the old depot
  And the train come rolling by,
  I looked in the window, saw the woman I loved,
  Bowed down my head and cried,
     Bowed down my head and cried, poor boy,
     Bowed down my head and cried,
     I looked in the window, saw the woman I loved,
     Bowed down my head and cried.

4 The jury found me guilty,
  The clerk, he wrote it down,
  The judge, he passed the sentence, poor boy,
  And I'm penitentiary bound,
     And I'm penitentiary bound, poor boy, *etc.*

6 I sit here in my prison cell,
  A-doin' the best I can,
  A-thinkin' about that woman I loved,
  She ran away with another man,
     She ran away with another man, poor boy, *etc.*

*A ·44-calibre pistol.

Jailbirds and hoboes from coast to coast have harmonized on this lugubrious American variant of the Anglo-Irish ballad, *The Boston Burglar.*

89. FRANKIE AND JOHNNY

1 Frankie and Johnny were lovers,
   Lordy, how they could love,
   Swore to be true to each other,
   True as the stars above,
       He was her man, but he done her wrong.

2 Little Frankie was a good gal,
   As everybody knows,
   She did all the work around the house,
   And pressed her Johnny's clothes,
       He was her man, but he done her wrong.

3 Johnny was a yeller man,
   With coal black, curly hair,
   Everyone up in St Louis
   Thought he was a millionaire,
       He was her man, but he done her wrong.

4 Frankie went down to the bar-room,
   Called for a bottle of beer,
   Says, 'Looky here, Mister Bartender,
   Has my lovin' Johnny been here?
       He is my man, and he's doin' me wrong.'

5 'I will not tell you no story,
   I will not tell you no lie.
   Johnny left here about an hour ago,
   With a gal named Nelly Bly,
       He is your man and he's doing you wrong.'

6 Little Frankie went down Broadway,
   With her pistol in her hand,
   Said, 'Stand aside you chorus gals,
   I'm lookin' for my man,
       He is my man, and he's doin' me wrong.'

7 The first time she shot him, he staggered,
   The next time she shot him, he fell,
   The last time she shot, O Lawdy,
   There was a new man's face in hell,
       She shot her man, for doin' her wrong.

8 'Turn me over doctor,
   Turn me over slow,
   I got a bullet in my left hand side,
   Great God, it's hurtin' me so.
       I was her man, but I done her wrong.'

9 It was a rubber-tyred buggy,
   Decorated hack,
   Took poor Johnny to the graveyard,
   Brought little Frankie back,
       He was her man, but he done her wrong.

10 It was not murder in the first degree,
   It was not murder in the third,
   A woman simply dropped her man
   Like a hunter drops his bird,
       She shot her man, for doin' her wrong.

11 The last time I saw Frankie,
   She was sittin' in the 'lectric chair,
   Waitin' to go and meet her God
   With the sweat runnin' out of her hair,
       She shot her man, for doin' her wrong.

12 Walked on down Broadway,
   As far as I could see,
   All I could hear was a two string bow
   Playin' *'Nearer my God to thee,'*
       He was her man, and he done her wrong.

No one knows the origins of Frankie and Johnny, the most popular and widely sung of American ballads. Various authorities have located the fatal shooting in Toe River, Tennessee; Louisville, Kentucky; Vickburg, Mississippi; and St Louis, Missouri. It is probably a Mississippi valley product from the pre-blues period of the 1890s for it closely resembles *Brady* and the *Boll Weevil* and other ballads of the same region and date. As the song became the favourite of college students and bar-room minstrels, it has tended to lose the tragic character of the Negro original, and to become a tragi-comic period piece.

90. BRADY AND DUNCAN

Slowly. With strong rhythm ♩=160

* These notes are between F♮ and F♯

CHORUS: 'Bra- dy, Bra- dy, Bra- dy, don't you know you done wrong,—
1. Dun- can, Dun- can was tend- in' bar,—— When

Com- in' in my groc-'ry when my game was go- in' on? Sprung-a my lock an' you
in walked Bra- dy with a shin- in' star, 'Dun- can, Dun- can, you

broke-a my bo',— Now you're ly- in' dead on my groc-'ry flo'.—
ur- der ar- rest',— And Dun- can shot a hole in Bra- dy's breast.—

CHORUS: '*Brady, Brady, Brady, don't you know you done wrong,*
Comin' in my groc'ry when my game was goin' on?
Sprung-a my lock an' you broke-a my bo', *
Now you're lyin' dead on my groc'ry flo'.' †

1 Duncan, Duncan was tendin' bar,
When in walked Brady with a shinin' star,
'Duncan, Duncan, you under arrest,'
And Duncan shot a hole in Brady's breast. *(Chorus)*

2 When the women heard that Brady was dead,
They went back home and outed in red,
Come slippin' and slidin' up and down the street,
In their loose Mother Hubbards and their stockin' feet. *(Chorus)*

3 Mrs Brady come in with a mighty flirt,
Wiped up the blood with her underskirt,
Says, 'Quit cryin', children, and hold your breath,
You'll all draw a pension at your daddy's death.' *(Chorus)*

4 Heard a mighty rumblin' way under the ground,
Must a-been Brady bound to Hell-town,
'Mama, mama, now what is that?'
'Brady's struttin' in Hell with his Stetson hat.' *(Chorus)*

*Bolt.
†Floor.

Coming out of the same Mississippi Valley honkey-tonks, gambling dens, and lowdown dance halls that nurtured the growth of jazz and blues, this ballad is even rowdier and jazzier than *Frankie and Johnnie*. It must be sung to a heavy jazz beat, blueing the notes, maintaining a fast blues tempo.

91. TAKE A SNIFF ON ME (THE COCAINE SONG)

1 Goin' up State Street, comin' down Main,
Lookin' for the woman that use cocaine.
Hi, Hi, baby, take a sniff on me,
All you bummers take a sniff on me,
Take a *! on me, take a *! on me,
An' a Hi, Hi, honey take a *! on me.

2 Woke up this mornin' by the courthouse bell,
Boys uptown givin' cocaine hell. *(Chorus)*

3 Went to Mister Lehman's on a lope,
Sign in the window said *No mo coke.* *(Chorus)*

4 You bring a nickel and I'll bring a dime,
You buy the coke and I'll buy the wine. *(Chorus)*

5 I chew my tobacco and I spit my juice,
And I love my baby till it ain't no use. *(Chorus)*

6 Cocaine's for horses and not for men,
The doctors say it'll kill you, but they don't say when. *(Chorus)*

7 Whifforee and a whifforye,
Gonna keep a-whiffin' boys, till I die. *(Chorus)*

8 Now the cocaine habit is mighty bad,
It kill everybody I know it to have had. *(Chorus)*

*Sing it or sniff it.

Half a century ago the sale of narcotics was not very strictly regulated in the south-western states. Negro levee camp workers could buy a box of cocaine tablets in the commissary, just as they might buy a bottle of whiskey, and they chewed the tabs as a cheap substitute for drink, before they quite realized the drug was habit-forming and destructive. Set to a ragtime air, this genuine 'snowbird' ballad was recorded by John A. Lomax and Alan Lomax in Texas penitentiaries.

92. DELIA

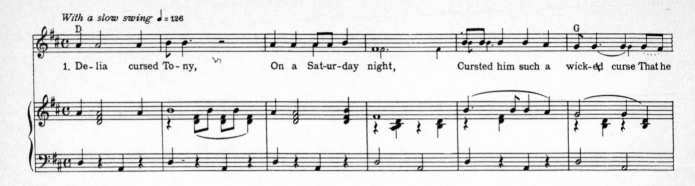

With a slow swing ♩ = 126

1. De-lia cursed To-ny, On a Sat-ur-day night, Cursted him such a wick-ed curse That he

CHORUS

swore he'd take her life, De-lia's gone, One more round, De-lia's gone.

2. The *etc.*

1 Delia cursed Tony,
On a Saturday night,
Cursted him such a wicked curse
That he swore he'd take her life,
Delia's gone,
One more round,
Delia's gone.

2 The first time he shot her,
Shot her in the side,
The second time he shot her,
She bowed her head and died. *(Chorus)*

3 They sent for the doctor,
He came dressed in black,
Done everything a doctor could do,
But he couldn't bring Delia back. *(Chorus)*

4 Monday he was 'rested,
Tuesday he was tried,
The jury found him guilty,
And the judge said, 'Ninety-nine.' *(Chorus)*

5 'Ninety-nine years in the prison,
Judge, that ain't no time,
I've got a brother in New Orleans
With nine hundred and ninety-nine.' *(Chorus)*

6 Now Tony he's in the jailhouse,
Drinkin' out a silver cup,
Delia she's in the graveyard,
Tryin' her best to get up. *(Chorus)*

7 'Jailer, O Jailer,
How can I sleep?
When all around my bedside,
My little Delia creeps.' *(Chorus)*

Delia, first cousin to *Frankie and Johnny*, is said to have met her fate in Dallas, Texas; the jazzy ballad, however, is best known on the eastern Sea-board, and in Nassau in the Bahamas, where it is still a popular song among street musicians.

93. THE MIDNIGHT SPECIAL

1 Yonder come Miss Rosie,
   How'n the world d'you know?
   Well, I knows her by her apron
   And the dress she wo',
   Umbereller on her shoulder,
   Piece of paper in her hand,
   Well, she come to tell the gov'nor,
   'Turn loose-a my man.'
   Let the midnight special shine its light on me,
   Let the midnight special shine its everlovin' light on me.

2 Well, you wake up in the mornin',
   When the ding dong ring,
   Go marchin' to the table,
   See the same damn thing.
   Knife and fork-a on the table,
   Nothin' in my pan,
   If you say anything about it,
   Haves trouble with the man. *(Chorus)*

3 If you ever go to Houston
   Boys, you better walk right,
   Well, you better not stumble
   And you better not fight.
   Cause the police will arrest you,
   And they'll carry you down,
   You can bet your bottom dollar,
   'Penitentiary bound'. *(Chorus)*

4 Now one of these mornin's
   And the time ain't long,
   That man's gonna call me,
   And I'll be gone.
   I'll be done all my grievin',
   Whoopin', holl'in', cryin',
   I'll be done all my worryin'
   'Bout my great long time. *(Chorus)*

As the headlight of a crack cross-continent train bores through the night past the Texas penitentiary, a Negro prisoner dreams of freedom. In his fancy he sees his sweetheart coming with his pardon. He thinks of the hard, monotonous prison life, of the ease with which a Negro without friends can land in jail, then he yearns again for a free life beyond the prison bars. This Texas convict lament, sung in harmony, is one of the most appealing of American folk songs. We found it in the Texas prisons in 1933-4.

94. THE OLD '97

1. Up on the moun-tain one cold frost-y morn-in', Just watch-in' the smoke from be-low, It was whirl-in' up from a short, black smoke-stack Way down on the Sou-thern Rail - road. turned.

1 Up on the mountain one cold frosty mornin',
Just watchin' the smoke from below,
It was whirlin' up from a short, black smokestack
Way down on the Southern Railroad.

2 It was the old '97, the fastest mailtrain,
That runs on the Southern Line,
And when she pulled into Monroe, Virginia,
She was forty-seven minutes behind.

3 They give him his orders in Monroe, Virginia,
Saying, 'Steve, you're way behind time.
It's not '38 it's old '97,
You must put her in Danville on time.'

4 'Just one more trip,' said the sleepy conductor,
As he kissed his loving wife,
'I've stole enough money from the railroad comp'ny
To last us all through life.'

5 'Goodbye, sweet wife,' said the drunken brakeman,
As he waved his cap with delight,
'If the wheels will roll and the engineer stays sober,
We'll all reach home tonight.'

6 Steve turned to his black and greasy fireman,
Said, 'Shovel in a little more coal,
And when we cross the White Oak mountain,
You can watch old '97 roll.'

7 He was going down the grade, makin' ninety miles an hour,
When his whistle broke into a scream,
He was found in the wreck with his hand on the throttle,
And scalded to death with the steam.

8 O, a sad farewell, when we heard the signal,
And the brakeman dropped the pin,
And for hours and hours the switchman waited
For the train that will never pull in.

9 Young ladies, you must take warning
From this time now and on,
Never speak harsh words to your true-lovin' husband,
He will leave you and never return.

10 Did she ever return? No, she never returned,
Though the train was due at one,
For hours and hours the watchman stood waitin'
For the train that never returned.

In the 1920s the Victor Gramophone Company published a version of *The Old '97*, done in hillbilly style with train effects; and the record sold several million copies. A few months later, a Virginia mountaineer, claiming that he was the composer, sued Victor for a million dollars. The mountaineer lost his case in the Supreme Court, as America's best ballad sleuth proved that the claimant had merely recomposed one of a chain of variants of an older ballad. It recalls the early days of American railroading, when wrecks and train robberies were everyday occurrences. No. 97, a fast mail train on the Southern Railroad, running between Washington and Atlanta, plunged off a curving trestle at the foot of White Oak mountain, near Danville, Va., on 27 September 1903. The train was destroyed and the crew killed.

95. CASEY JONES

1 Some folks say Casey Jones can't run,
Stop and listen what Casey done,
He left Memphis at a quarter to nine,
Made Newport News 'fore dinner time,
'Fore dinner time, 'fore dinner time,
Made Newport News 'fore dinner time.

2 Casey Jones, before he died,
Fixed the blinds so the bums couldn' ride,
'If they ride, gotta ride the rod,
Trust their life in the hands of God.
In the hands of God, the hands of God,
Trust their life in the hands of God.'

3 There was a woman named Alice Fly,
Said, 'I'm gonna ride with Mr Casey or die,
I ain't good lookin' but I takes my time,
I'm a ramblin' woman with a ramblin' mind,
With a ramblin' mind,' etc.

4 Early one mornin', 'bout four o'clock,
Told his fireman, 'Get the boiler hot,
All I need's a little water and coal,
Peep out my window, see the drivers roll,
See the drivers roll, etc.

5 He looked at his watch and his watch was slow,
He looked at the water and the water was low.
But the people all knew by the engine's moan,
That the man at the throttle was Casey Jones,
Was Casey Jones, etc.

6 When he come within a mile of the place,
Old Number Four stared him right in the face.
Told his fireman, 'Just keep your seat and ride,
It's a double track road, running side by side,
Runnin' side by side,' etc.

7 You ought to been there to see the sight,
Screamin' an' cryin', both coloured and white,
And I was a witness for the fact,
They flagged Mister Casey, but he never looked back,
But he never looked back, etc.

8 'Mama, mama have you heard the news,
Papa got killed on the C.B. and Qs'*
'Quit cryin', children, and don't do that,
You've got another papa on the same durn track,
On the same durn track,' etc.

*The Cincinnati, Burlington, and Quincy Railroad

Casey Jones, a dare-devil Irish-American engine driver, was killed in a wreck on the Illinois Central Line, south of Memphis, Tennessee, on the night of 29 April 1906. Wallace Saunders, a Negro helper in the roundhouse at Canton, Mississippi, cleaned up the engine in which Casey was killed; and it was he who set the Casey Jones ballad on its way by putting Casey's name into an older railroad ballad about 'po' Jimmy Jones, the good old porter'. Here you have the Mississippi folk song that grew up out of Saunders' fragment, which we recorded in Canton in 1933. The better known and much less beautiful version, was composed by two white vaudevillians who heard the Saunders ballad and made Casey Jones into an early Tin Pan Alley hit.

96. THE ROCK ISLAND LINE

CHORUS: *O the Rock Island Line is a mighty good road,*
Yes, the Rock Island Line is the road to ride,
Well, the Rock Island Line is a mighty good road,
If you want to ride it, got to ride it like you flyin',
Buy your ticket at the station on the Rock Island Line.

1 She's comin' down the track just runnin' like hell,
  Blowin' her whistle and ringin' her bell. *(Chorus)*

2 She left St Louis at a quarter to nine,
  Got to Fort Worth, Texas, 'fo' dinner time. *(Chorus)*

3 I may be right and I may be wrong,
  I know you're gonna miss me when I'm gone. *(Chorus)*

4 A, B, C double X, Y, Z,
  The cat's in the corner and it can't see me. *(Chorus)*

John A. Lomax recorded this song at the Cumins State Prison Farm, Gould, Arkansas, in 1934 from its convict composer, Kelly Pace. The Negro singer, Leadbelly, heard it, rearranged it in his own style, and made commercial phonograph recordings of it in the forties. One of these recordings was studied and imitated phrase by phrase, by a young English singer of American folk songs, who subsequently recorded it for an English company. The record sold in the hundreds of thousands in the U.S. and England, and this Arkansas Negro convict song, as adapted by Leadbelly, was published as a personal copyright, words and music, by someone whose contact with the Rock Island Line was entirely through the grooves of a phonograph record.

97. HALLELUJAH, I'M A BUM

With a hearty swing ♩ = 152

When spring-time has come, O won't we have fun, We'll git out of jail, And we'll go on the bum. Hal-le-

-lu-jah, I'm a bum, Hal-le-lu-jah, bum a-gain, Hal-le-lu-jah, give us a hand-out, To re-vive us a-gain.

1 When springtime has come,
O won't we have fun,
We'll git out of jail,
And we'll go on the bum.
Hallelujah, I'm a bum,
Hallelujah, bum again,
Hallelujah, give us a handout,
To revive us again.

2 O why don't you work,
Like other men do?
O how can I work,
When the sky is so blue? *(Chorus)*

3 I went to a house,
And I knocked on the door,
The lady says, 'Bum, bum,
You been here before.' *(Chorus)*

4 I called on another,
And asked for some bread,
The lady says, 'Bum, bum,
The baker is dead.' *(Chorus)*

5 I'll ride the box cars,
And hop the fast mails,
When it's cold in the winter
I'll sleep in the jails. *(Chorus)*

6 If I was to work,
And save all I earn,
I'd buy me a bar,
And have money to burn. *(Chorus)*

7 Someday a freight train
Will run over my head,
And the sawbones will say,
'Old One Finger's dead.' *(Chorus)*

The half century between 1880 and 1930 were the palmy days of the American tramp. He suffered often from hunger and exposure, but he escaped the priggishness and Babbitry of the period. Above all, he was free to travel where he liked; for him the whistle of a fast freight was an invitation to the unknown and to adventure. Thus, round the campfires in the hobo jungles, ballads were composed and passed on by word of mouth, which thumbed the nose at the lives of stable, hard-working folk. Like many a hobo song, this, too, is an ironic parody of a Baptist hymn – in this instance, *Hallelujah, Thine the Glory*.

98. THE BIG ROCK CANDY MOUNTAINS

130

CHORUS
give a little

Big Rock Can - dy Moun - tains. O ___ the ___ buz-zin' of the bees In the

ci - ga - rette trees, Round the so - da - wa - ter foun - tains, Near the le - mon - ade springs, where the

whang-doo-dle sings In the Big Rock Can - dy Moun - tains. 2. In the *etc.* Moun - tains.

repeats to Verses | *last time*

INTRO. On a summer day in the month of May,
A burly little bum come a-hikin',
He was travelin' down that lonesome road,
A-lookin' for his likin'.
He was headed for a land that's far away,
Beside those crystal fountains,
'I'll see you all, this comin' fall
In the Big Rock Candy Mountains.'

1 In the Big Rock Candy Mountains
You never change your socks,
And the little streams of alkyhol
Come a-tricklin' down the rocks.
Where the shacks all have to tip their hats,
And the railroad bulls* are blind,
There's a lake of stew, and whiskey, too,
And you can paddle all around 'em in your big canoe,
In the Big Rock Candy Mountains.
O . . . the . . . buzzin' of the bees
In the cigarette trees,
Round the sodawater fountains,
Near the lemonade springs,
Where the whangdoodle sings
In the Big Rock Candy Mountains.

2 In the Big Rock Candy Mountains,
There's a land that's fair and bright,
Where the handouts grow on bushes,
And you sleep out every night.
Where the box cars are all empty
And the sun shines every day,
O I'm bound to go, where there ain't no snow,
Where the rain don't fall and the wind don't blow,
In the Big Rock Candy Mountains. *(Chorus)*

3 In the Big Rock Candy Mountains,
The jails are made of tin,
And you can bust right out again
As soon as they put you in.
The farmers' trees are full of fruit,
The barns are full of hay,
I'm goin' to stay where you sleep all day,
Where they boiled in oil the inventor of toil,
In the Big Rock Candy Mountains. *(Chorus)*

*Railroad guards.

A recent study indicates that the American hobo fantasy may be an offshoot of the Celtic myths of the Western Isles, where the heroes of Irish folklore lived on after death, and of the medieval legends of the land of Cockaigne. It was with such fabrications – indeed, with this very song – that the professional tramp, looking for a young punk to 'keep house' for him on his travels, used to induce farm lads to run away from home and join him on the road.

131

99. ABDUL THE BUL BUL AMEER

1. The sons of the pro-phet were har-dy and bold,_____ And quite un-ac-cus-tomed to fear,_____ But the bra-vest of all was the man I re-call As Ab-dul, the Bul Bul A-meer._____ 2. If you ___ etc.

1 The sons of the prophet were hardy and bold,
   And quite unaccustomed to fear,
   But the bravest of all was the man I recall
   As Abdul, the Bul Bul Ameer.

2 If you wanted a man to encourage the van,
   Or to harass the foe in the rear,
   Or to storm a redoubt, you would set up a shout
   For Abdul, the Bul Bul Ameer.

3 There were heroes in plenty and men known to fame,
   Who fought in the ranks of the Tsar,
   But the bravest of all was the man by the name
   Of Ivan Skizavinsky Skivar.

4 He could sing like Caruso, tell fortunes by cards,
   And play on the Spanish guitar,
   O yes, quite the cream of the Muscoviteen
   Was Ivan Skizavinsky Skivar.

5 One day this bold Muscovite shouldered his gun,
   And walked on the streets with a sneer,
   He was looking for fun when he happened to run
   On Abdul, the Bul Bul Ameer.

6 'Young man', said Bul Bul, 'Is existence so dull
   That you're anxious to end your career?
   For infidel, know you have trod on the toe
   Of Abdul, the Bul Bul Ameer.

7 'So take your last look at the sunshine and brook
   And send your regrets to the Tsar,
   By which I imply, you are going to die,
   Mister Ivan Skizavinsky Skivar.'

8 Then that brave Mameluke drew his trusty skabook,
   Crying, 'Allah il Allah Akbar.'
   And with murderous intent, he most suddenly went
   At Ivan Skizavinsky Skivar.

9 The whistling skabook did like lightning descend
   And caught Ivan right over the ear,
   While the sabre of Ivan pressed right through the heart
   Of Abdul, the Bul Bul Ameer.

10 The Sultan rode up the disturbance to quell,
   And to give to the victor a cheer,
   But arrived just in time to take a hasty farewell
   Of Abdul, the Bul Bul Ameer.

11 Then Gotchikoff, Skabeloff, Metchnikoff, too,
   Drove up in the Emperor's car,
   But only in time to bid hasty adieu,
   To Ivan Skizavinsky Skivar.

12 On the banks of a stream where the cold Dnieper flows,
   There is written in characters clear,
   'O stranger remember and pray for the soul
   Of Abdul, the Bul Bul Ameer.'

13 While a Muscovite maiden her vigil doth keep,
   By the light of the cold Northern star,
   And the name that she constantly shrieks in her sleep,
   Is Ivan Skizavinsky Skivar.

A whole school of fantastical ballads were produced and handed on orally among American college students in the early years of the twentieth century. By far the best was this satirical portrait of the soldier of fortune, the hero of so many romantic novels of the period.

100. CARELESS LOVE

1. It's on this railroad bank I stand, _____ It's on this railroad bank I stand, _____ on this railroad bank I stand, _____ All for the love of a railroad man.

love, oh love, oh care-less love, _____ love, oh love, oh care-less love, _____ love, oh care-less love, _____ You see what care-less love will do.

1 It's on this railroad bank I stand,
  It's on this railroad bank I stand,
  It's on this railroad bank I stand,
  All for the love of a railroad man.
      It's love, oh love, oh careless love,
      It's love, oh love, oh careless love,
      It's love, oh love, oh careless love,
      You see what careless love will do.

2 I love my mama and my papa too, *(three times)*
  I'd leave them both for lovin' you. *(Chorus)*

3 Sorrow, sorrow to my heart *(twice)*
  O it's sorrow, sorrow to my heart,
  Since my true love and I did part. *(Chorus)*

4 I cried last night and the night before, *(three times)*
  I'll cry tonight and cry no more. *(Chorus)*

5 Lord, I wish that train would come, *(twice)*
  How I wish that train would come
  And take me back where I come from. *(Chorus)*

6 When my apron strings did bow, *(three times)*
  You followed me through sleet and snow. *(Chorus)*

7 Now my apron strings won't pin, *(three times)*
  You pass my door and don't look in. *(Chorus)*

Some early blues ran to sixteen bars and four lines. The twelve-bar, three-line blues was a later development. *Careless Love* and *Make me a Pallet on your Floor*, two very similar sixteen-bar blues, are regarded by old timers in the Mississippi Delta as the 'first blues'. *Careless Love* is also an 'old' Southern white folk song, with roots in the British lyric tradition, indicating the strong undercurrent of white influence in the original blues. This is a mountain version of the Negro song.

101. ST JAMES INFIRM'RY

1. I went down to the St James Infirm'ry.
   My baby, there she lay,
   Laid out on a cold marble table,
   Well, I looked and I turned away.
   'What is my baby's chances?'
   I ask'd old Doctor Sharp,
   'Boy, by six o'clock this evenin',
   She'll be playin' her golden harp.'
   Let her go, let her go, God bless her,
   Wherever she may be,
   She can hunt this wide world over,
   But she'll never find a man like me.

2. Sixteen coal-black horses,
   Hitched to a rubber-tired hack,
   Carried seven girls to the graveyard,
   And brought only six of them back.
   Now when I die, please bury me,
   In my milk-white Stetson hat,
   With afive-dollar gold piece on mywatch chain,
   So they'll know I died standin' pat. *(Chorus)*

3. Six poker dealers for pall bearers,
   Let a whore sing my funeral song,
   With a red hot band just beatin' it out,
   Raisin' hell as we roll along.
   Now I may be drowned in the ocean,
   May be killed by the cannonball,
   But let me tell you, buddy,
   A woman was the cause of it all. *(Chorus)*

One of the British songs most productive of American variants is the eighteenth-century stall ballad, *The Unfortunate Rake*, which celebrates the gaudy and bawdy funeral of a soldier who died of syphilis. American singers censored the song in creating the Western *Street of Laredo*, and the jazzy blues tune, *St James Infirm'ry*, collected by John A. Lomax in the early 1900s.

102. THE RISING SUN

1 There is a house in New Orleans,
They call the Rising Sun,
It's been the ruin of many a poor girl,
And me, O God, for one.

2 Go tell my baby sister,
Never do like I have done,
Tell her to shun that house in New Orleans,
They call the Rising Sun.

3 If I'd a listened what my mama said,
I'd-a been at home today,
Being so young and foolish, poor boy,
Let a rambler lead me astray.

4 My mother, she's a tailor,
She made those new blue jeans,
My sweetheart he's a drunkard, Lord, Lord,
Drinks down in New Orleans.

5 The only thing a drunkard needs
Is a suitcase and a trunk,
The only time he's satisfied
Is when he's on a drunk.

6 Fills his glasses to the brim
And passes them around,
The only pleasure he gets outa life,
Is ramblin' from town to town.

7 One foot is on the platform,
The other one on the train,
Im goin' back to New Orleans
To wear that ball and chain.

8 Goin' back to New Orleans,
My race is almost run,
Goin' to spend the rest of my life,
Beneath the Rising Sun.

A ragged Kentucky Mountain girl recorded this modern Southern white song for me in 1937 in Middlesborough, Kentucky, the hardboiled town in the Cumberland Gap on the Tennessee border. This blues song of a lost girl probably derives from some older British piece. At any rate, the house of the Rising Sun occurs in several *risqué* English songs, and the melody is one of several for the ancient and scandalous ballad *Little Musgrave*.

135

103. THE TITANIC

1 O they built the ship Titanic to sail the ocean blue,
And they thought they had a ship that the water would never leak through,
But the Lord Almighty's hand knew this ship would never stand,
It was sad when that great ship went down.
It was sad, it was sad,
It was sad when that great ship went down,
Husbands and wives, little children lost their lives,
It was sad when that great ship went down.

2 O they sailed from England and were almost to the shore,
When the rich refused to associate with the poor,
So they put them down below, where they were the first to go.
(Chorus)

3 The Titanic left the harbour at a rapid speed,
She was carrying everything that the peoples need,
She sailed six hundred miles away, met an icebug on her way,
(Chorus)

4 It was on a Monday morning just about four o'clock,
When the ship Titanic felt that terrible shock,
People began to scream and cry, sayin' 'Lord, am I going to die?'
(Chorus)

5 The boat was full of sin and the sides about to burst,
When the captain shouted, 'A-women and children first.'
O the captain tried to wire, but the lines were all on fire,
(Chorus)

6 Now the ship began to settle and they all tried to flee,
And the band it struck up, 'Nearer My God to Thee',
And Death came ridin' by, sixteen hundred had to die,
(Chorus)

When the *Titanic*, the greatest ocean liner built up to that time, struck an iceberg and went down on her maiden voyage in 1912, the simple folk of the South took it as a religious warning. A rumour circulated among Negroes that Jack Johnson, the coloured heavyweight champion, had been refused passage. A number of street-balladiers composed and circulated Titanic ballads, all with a note of religious warning. With time, an intentionally comic, hillbilly version has become widely popular.

104. WORRIED MAN

CHORUS: *It takes a worried man to sing a worried song,*
It takes a worried man to sing a worried song,
It takes a worried man to sing a worried song,
I'm worried now but I won't be worried long.

1 I went across the river, and I laid down to sleep, *(three times)*
  When I woke up, I had shackles on my feet. *(Chorus)*

2 Twenty-nine links of chain around my leg, *(three times)*
  And on each link, the initials of my name. *(Chorus)*

3 I asked the judge what might be my fine, *(three times)*
  Twenty-one years on the R.C. Mountain line. *(Chorus)*

4 The train arrived, sixteen coaches long, *(three times)*
  The girl I love is on that train and gone. *(Chorus)*

5 If anyone asks you who composed this song, *(three times)*
  Tell him 'twas I, and I sing it all day long. *(Chorus)*

The most prolific and spontaneous song-maker in modern America is the hillbilly – the last American to become urbanized – the Southern mountaineer who comes to town, gets a job in the mill, buys a guitar and adapts his ancient traditional heritage of song to city standards. Today, commercial hillbilly music is heard everywhere, on records, in films, and via the radio and television. The genuine hillbilly folksongs, such as *Worried Man*, *Birmingham Jail*, and others, have become a permanent part of the American folksong repertoire, appealing precisely because they are hybrids, showing British, Negro, and urban popular song influences.

105. IRENE

CHORUS: *Irene, good-night,*
Irene, good-night,
Good-night, Irene, good-night, Irene,
I'll kiss you in my dreams.

1 I asked your mother for you,
She told me you were too young,
I wish to the Lawd I'd never seen your face,
I'm sorry you ever was born. *(Chorus)*

2 Last Saturday night I got married,
Me an' my wife settled down,
Now me an' my wife have parted,
Gonna take me a stroll uptown. *(Chorus)*

3 Quit ramblin' an' quit gamblin',
Quit stayin' out late at night,
Stay home with your wife an' your fam'ly,
Sit down by the fireside bright. *(Chorus)*

4 I love Irene, God knows I do,
Love her till the sea runs dry,
And if Irene turns her back on me,
I'm gonna take morphine and die. *(Chorus)*

5 Sometimes I lives in the country,
Sometimes I lives in town,
Sometimes I has a great notion,
Of jumpin' into the river an' drown. *(Chorus)*

Huddie Ledbetter (Leadbelly), was born in 1885 in Mooringsport, La., and died in 1950 in New York City. He has already passed into legend as the great American folk singer. A man of incredible physique and fiery temperament, he was equally renowned among his people as worker, twelve-string guitarist, and singer. He spent years in prison for serious crimes, but literally sang his way out of two Southern penitentiaries, his ballads gaining pardons for him. He was the first singer we recorded for the Library of Congress in the summer of 1933 and *Irene*, which he had learned from an uncle and had made popular in both Texas and Louisiana in his own arrangement, was the first song.

138

106. WHICH SIDE ARE YOU ON?

1 Come all of you good workers,
   Good news to you I'll tell,
   Of how the good old union
   Has come in here to dwell.
   Which side are you on,
   Tell me, which side are you on?

2 My daddy was a miner,
   He's now in the air an' sun,
   Stick with him, brother miners,
   Until this battle's won. *(Chorus)*

3 They say in Harlan county,
   There are no neutrals there,
   You'll either be a union man,
   Or a thug for J. H. Blair. *(Chorus)*

4 O gentlemen, can you stand it,
   O tell me if you can,
   Will you be a lousy scab,
   Or will you be a man? *(Chorus)*

5 Don't scab for the bosses,
   Don't listen to their lies,
   Us workers haven't got a chance,
   Unless we organize. *(Chorus)*

Florence Reece, a shy, towheaded Kentucky miner's daughter, composed this song at the age of twelve when her father was out on strike. She sang it to me standing in front of the primitive hearth of a log cabin in the back-woods of Kentucky in 1937 and it has since become a national union song. The tune is an American variant of the English *Jack Munro*, 'which side are you on' having been substituted for 'lay the lily-o'.

107. BLOWIN' DOWN THE ROAD

Rather fast, with vitality ♩ = 120

1. Well, I'm blow-in' down that old dust-y road, Lawd, Lawd, Yes, I'm blow-in' down that old dust-y road, Yes, I'm blow-in' down that old dust-y road, Lawd, Lawd, An' I ain't a-gon-na be treat-ed this-a-way. *repeats* 2. Well, I'm *etc.* way. *Finis*

1 Well, I'm blowin' down that old dusty road, Lawd, Lawd,
  Yes, I'm blowin' down that old dusty road,
  Yes, I'm blowin' down that old dusty road, Lawd, Lawd,
  An' I ain't a-gonna be treated this-a-way.

2 Well, I'm goin' where the climate suits my clothes, Lawd, Lawd,
  Yes, I'm goin' where the climate suits my clothes,
  Yes, I'm goin' where the climate suits my clothes, Lawd, Lawd,
  I'm goin' where them chilly winds don't blow.

3 Well, I'm goin' where the water tastes like wine, Lawd, Lawd,
  Yes, I'm goin' where the water tastes like wine,
  Yes, I'm goin' where the water tastes like wine, Lawd, Lawd,
  Lord, this New York* water tastes like turpentine.

4 Who'll stir your gravy when I'm gone, Lawd, Lawd,
  Who'll stir your gravy when I'm gone,
  Who'll stir your gravy when I'm gone, Lawd, Lawd,
  When I'm gone down that long lonesome road?

5 It takes a ten-dollar shoe to fit my feet, Lawd, Lawd,
  It takes a ten-dollar shoe to fit my feet,
  It takes a ten-dollar shoe to fit my feet, Lawd, Lawd,
  An' I ain't gonna be treated this-a-way.

6 I ain't got but one old lousy dime, Lawd, Lawd,
  I ain't got but one old lousy dime,
  I ain't got but one old lousy dime, Lawd, Lawd,
  But I'll find me a new dollar some old day.

7 I'm goin' where the orange blossoms blow, Lawd, Lawd,
  Yes, I'm goin' where the orange blossoms blow,
  Yes, I'm goin' where the orange blossoms blow, Lawd, Lawd,
  An' I ain't a-gonna be treated this-a-way.

*Give the name of any place.

This is the great folk song of the depression and New Deal period. In form and origin it is a Negro blues, but millions of Okies, Arkies, southern 'crackers', all homeless and jobless, made it the blues of the *Grapes of Wrath* people. It can be sung solo with guitar; it makes a good square-dance tune for fiddle, guitar, and banjo; and it sounds fine with three-part harmony, hymn-style.

108. SO LONG

1. I'll sing you a song and I'll sing it again,
   Of the place that I lived on, the dry, wind-y plain, In the
   month of A-pril, in the coun-ty called Clay, And here's what all of the peo-ple there say, they said,

CHORUS

So long, it's been good to know you, So long, it's been good to know you, So long, it's
been good to know you, This dust-y old dust is a-get-tin' my home, And I've got to be drift-in' a-long.

1 I'll sing you a song and I'll sing it again,
Of the place that I lived on the dry, windy plain,
In the month of April, in the county called Clay,
And here's what all of the people there say, they said,
   So long, it's been good to know you,
   So long, it's been good to know you,
   So long, it's been good to know you,
   This dusty old dust is a-gettin' my home,
   And I've got to be driftin' along.

2 That dust storm hit, and it hit like thunder,
It dusted us over and covered us under,
It blocked off the traffic and covered the sun,
And straight for home all the people did run, singing, *(Chorus)*

3 Two sweethearts set in the dark and they sparked,
They hugged and they kissed in the dusty old dark,
They sighed and cried and hugged and kissed,
Instead of marriage they talked like this, they said, *(Chorus)*

4 The telephone rang and it jumped off the wall,
That was the preacher, a-makin' his call,
He said 'Kind friends, this must be the end,
You've got your last chance at salvation from sin, then it's,' *(Chorus)*

5 The church was jammed, the church was packed,
That dusty old dust storm, it blowed so black,
The preacher could not read a word of his text,
So he folded his specks and he took up collection, singin', *(Chorus)*

Woody Guthrie is a ballad composer in the folk tradition of the anonymous folk poets who made *Jesse James*, *Gerry's Rocks*, and *The Buffalo Skinners*. The fact that his hundreds of songs reflect modern events and that he composes with a typewriter and a guitar only makes his achievement more unusual. He inherited the folk tradition of the last American frontier (western Oklahoma) and during his incessant wandering across the United States he has composed and recomposed this tradition into contemporary folky ballads about the lives of the American working class. Some of these songs have already passed into oral circulation. Many more will do so. No modern American poet or folk singer has made a more important contribution to our culture. This is one of his many songs about the experiences of his fellow Okies. The tune is a variant of Leadbelly's *Irene*.

141

109. ALABAMA BOUND

1 I'm Alabama bound, I'm Alabama bound, *(twice)*
Sho' as the train pulls out East today,
I'm Alabama bound. *(twice)*

2 Doncha leave me here, doncha leave me here *(twice)*
But if you just must go, just must go,
Leave me a dime for beer. *(twice)*

3 Way down the road somewhere, way down the road somewhere *(twice)*
I got a long, tall, teasin' brown,
Way down the road somewhere. *(twice)*

4 Now if that's your man, *(twice)*
Pin him to your side, *(twice)*
For if he mounts this train, O babe,
Sho' gonna let him ride. *(twice)*

5 Now you got a good man, *(twice)*
An' he won't treat you right, *(twice)*
Hit him in the head with the coal-oil lamp,
An' walk the streets all night. *(twice)*

6 If you got a good gal, *(twice)*
An' she won't treat you right, *(twice)*
Knock her down, stomp on her, cut her head,
An' walk the streets all night. *(twice)*

7 Why don't you be like me, *(twice)*
Why don't you be like me? *(twice)*
Drink yo' high tension whiskey, babe,
An' let yo' cocaine be. *(twice)*

8 I'm Alabama bound, I'm Alabama bound, *(twice)*
If the train don't run, I got a mule to ride,
I'm Alabama bound. *(twice)*

Perhaps nothing more than the euphony of the name prompted Negro blues singers to moan 'I'm Alabama bound'. This early folk blues catches the restless, adventurous spirit of the early 1900s when Negroes left the farm and wandered from job to job and town to town, looking for a better life and an escape from the confines of Southern prejudice. They lived in a harsh, violent world of honkey-tonks, gambling dens, and fast women, and their songs, which reflect the tough loneliness of that life, have become universally popular today now that a rapidly changing world has disrupted so many traditional patterns of life.

110. WANDERIN'

1 I been wanderin' early,
I been wanderin' late,
From New York City
To the Golden Gate.
And it looks like
I ain't never gonna cease my wanderin'.

2 I worked in the army,
  I worked on the farm,
  And all I've got to show's
  Just this muscle in my arm. *(Chorus)*

3 My daddy was an engineer,
  My brother drove a hack,
  My sister takes in washin'
  And the baby balls the jack.*

4 Whales in the ocean,
  Fish in the sea,
  A blonde-headed woman
  Made a monkey outa me. *(Chorus)*

*Popular dance step.

Carl Sandburg, the great American poet and ballad singer, found this haunting hobo lament in Minnesota. He chants it slowly and reflectively, with many pauses and a final rumbling downward release on the word *wanderin'*, as if a big, weary hobo had arrived at the Pearly Gates and was summing up his life story for St Peter. It can, however, be sung with a slow jazz beat to make a fine bluesy tune.

111. FARE THEE WELL, O HONEY (DINK'S SONG)

1 When I wo' my apron low,
   Couldn't keep you from my do'.
      Fare thee well, O honey,
      Fare thee well.

2 When I wo' my apron high,
   Sca'sely ever seed you passin' by. *(Chorus)*

3 When my apron come unpin,
   Pass my do' an' you wouldn' come in. *(Chorus)*

4 If I had a-lissened what mama said,
   I'd been a-sleepin' in mama's bed. *(Chorus)*

5 One of these days an' it won't be long,
   You'll call my name an' I'll be gone. *(Chorus)*

6 If I had wings like Noah's dove,
   I'd fly up the river to the man I love. *(Chorus)*

On a visit to a Brazos River levee camp in the early 1900s, John Lomax found a Negro woman with a remarkable voice, whose name was Dink. She felt shy of singing for him, but, encouraged by a pint of gin, she sang for Mrs. Lomax a four-line, unrhymed country blues, and then *Fare Thee Well,* which is part blues, part British lyric, and all perfection.

144

Appendix 1

AMERICAN FOLK GUITAR STYLE

AMERICAN FOLK GUITAR STYLE

1. GENERAL

The following pages present a brief account of one method for learning authentic accompaniments to American folk songs. It will serve as a guide for learners, but even skilful players may find some useful hints in the section on right-hand rhythms (Section 3).

Guitar position

Figure 1 illustrates one of the most comfortable methods of holding the guitar. The player is holding the neck of the guitar with the 'folk grip' – that is, with the neck resting in the palm of his hand. A more difficult, but perhaps ultimately a more satisfactory grip, is the classical Spanish position illustrated in Figure 2. A strap across the shoulders will enable you to play while standing.

1 The folk singer's position

2 The Classical or Spanish position

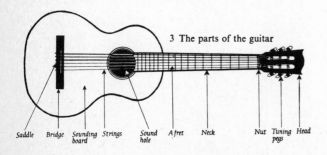

3 The parts of the guitar

Saddle Bridge Sounding Strings Sound A fret Neck Nut Tuning Head
                board   hole   pegs

Tuning

Figure 4 shows the guitar strings labelled from the fine tenor string to the heavy bass, E B G D A E. Beginning with the 'little E', tune your guitar at the piano as follows:

1 to the E above middle C
2 to the next B below middle C
3 to the next G below
4 to the next D below
5 to the next A below
6 to the next E below

To change the pitch of the strings to make chords or to play melodies, the player must press down on the strings with the ball

4 The position of the A7 chord

of the fingers between two frets, not touching the nearby strings and holding firmly so that there is no 'buzz' when the strings are plucked. For some chords you will have to press two strings at once with the flat of the finger. (See Figure 5.)

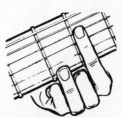

5 The strings of the guitar (left to right): E A D G B E

Practice

Practise every day, even if for a short time. Practise slowly so as to avoid mistakes. Always keep up a steady rhythm, even if it is quite slow at first. It is most important to trim the nails of the left hand short, and to file the nails of the right hand so that they are just even with the fingertips.

Divide your practice into three parts as follows:
(a) Right-hand exercise (Section 3); smooth, steady right-hand rhythm is the secret of folk playing.
(b) Learn the chords, following the diagrams in Section 2.
(c) Master the keyboard by picking out familiar melodies.
Then try out the songs in this book, following the arrangement of chords indicated by letter symbols above the treble clefs.

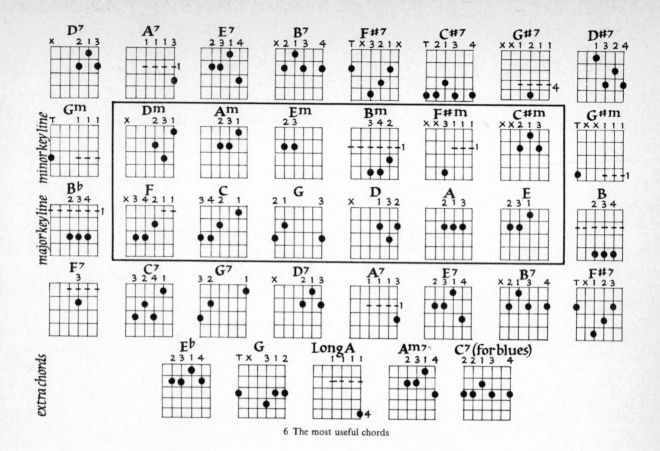

6 The most useful chords

2. THE CHORDS

In the diagrams (Figures 6, 7, and 8) the *black dots* indicate where the strings are to be fretted for each chord. The *broken lines* indicate that a finger is to be laid across two or more strings. The *numbers* tell which finger is used in each case. The x's are for strings not to be played within a chord. Where strings are un-labelled they are to be sounded within the chord. *T* indicates a string to be fretted with the thumb.

Figure 6 contains the chord families in major and minor of the keys of F C G D A and E, the six easiest and most useful keys for the guitar, when tuned as directed above.

Figures 7 and 8 show you how to use Figure 6, because in Figure 6 all the related chords in each key lie around the key chord in the same spatial relationship to it as those in Figures 7 and 8.

Major keys: Figure 7

Play C, then the chord to the left, next the chord below C, then C again. Repeat until you have the feeling of the key of C. Then try accompanying easy familiar songs limited to three chords. (You may find it easier to begin with the chord family related to E.) You can find the three main major chords in other keys by applying the method of this diagram to Figure 6.

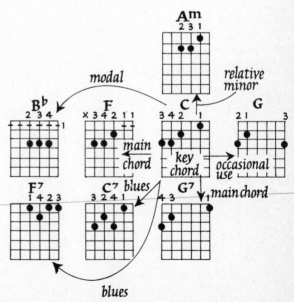

7 The related chords in the key of C major

148

Minor keys: Figure 8

Play A minor, then the chord to the left, next the chord above Am, then Am again. Repeat until you have the feeling of this minor key. You will notice that Am, the relative minor of C major, lies directly above it (see Figure 7). This relationship is true of all the major and minor chords. Many tunes in minor keys are included in this book.

(Note: Many songs move from major to minor, or the reverse, and it is therefore very important to practise relative major and minor chords.)

The blues

Referring to Figure 7, play C, then C7 diagonally below and to the left, then F directly above, then F7 diagonally below to the left, then C, the G7 directly below C, then C. This cycle of chords in various combinations will accompany most folk blues. The blues chords in other keys can be found by following the same pattern round the key chords.

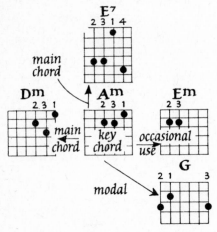

8 The related chords in the key of A minor

The older modal melodies

To accompany these, a few additional chords are required. These are indicated by the arrows labelled 'modal' and 'occasional use' in Figures 7 and 8. The additional chords required for modal playing may be found in all six keys in the same relationship to the key chords. In order to acquire a feeling for their use try out Nos. 15, 18, and 25 in this book.

Using the capo

The capo is a movable clamp which fits around the neck of the guitar and, when tightened, frets all the strings at a given fret. Each time it is moved up or down it changes the pitch of all the strings by half a tone.

The capo has two principal uses: (a) If you want to use a particular set of chords, but find the key doesn't suit the pitch of your voice, you can move the capo up the neck of the guitar one or several frets until the pitch suits you better. In the same way, if your instrument is tuned lower than another instrument with which you want to play, moving the capo up can put you quickly in pitch with that instrument, provided you are off by a measure of half steps. (b) The capo enables you to play in all twelve keys without the necessity of learning the fingering of all the chords for those keys. For example, if you wish to play in E flat, clamp your capo behind the first fret and play the chords of the D formation. If you then play your E formation chords you will be playing in F. If you move the capo up two frets from the bridge and play the C chords, you will actually be playing in D; if you play the A minor chords, you will actually be playing in the difficult key of B minor.

3. RIGHT-HAND RHYTHMS

American folk guitar gets its distinctive tone-colour largely from the various ways the right hand plucks and brushes the strings. Once you have learned a few chords, devote as much time as possible to right-hand rhythm. Try out the 'scratch' and the 'blues lick' (see below); if you find them easy, you will soon be playing in the Southern style. If this seems too difficult, begin with strumming and plucking.

Strumming

(a) For slow, non-rhythmic ballads, draw the thumb down across all the strings once or twice every line on the strong accents of the verse (Figure 9). This may, of course, be done in any rhythm one chooses.

(b) For songs in 2/4 or 4/4 time, pluck one of the bass strings with the thumb. Then stroke the three treble strings with the thumb. Repeat *ad lib* to the rhythm dah-di-dah-di.

(c) For songs in 3/4 or waltz time, pluck one of the bass strings with the thumb. Then stroke down across the three treble strings with the thumb twice. Repeat *ad lib* to the rhythm dah-di-di.

There are other ways of strumming, all useful to know, all good preparation for the more complex strokes to come. You can pluck with the thumb, then strum up across the treble strings with one finger, or with all the fingers (Figure 10). Or you can pluck with the thumb, then scratch down across the treble strings with the first finger or with all the fingers.

9 The thumb strum   10 Strumming with the fingers

Plucking

(a) Pluck with the thumb as described above, but to sound the treble strings place the first three fingers as in Figure 11, and pluck all three treble strings simultaneously in the rhythm you want. To get a good pluck, pull from slightly underneath, then across the string.

(b) To perform a rippling pluck or an arpeggio stroke, pluck with the thumb as before, then pluck each of the three treble strings in turn. This turns your dah-di, dah-di rhythm into dah-dle-di-di, dah-dle-di-di. For waltz time, the rhythm is dah-dle-di-di-di-di. One of the best accompaniments for American ballads is composed of alternating measures of straight pluck and arpeggio pluck – that is dah-di, dah-dle-di-di, etc.

(c) To play in 3/8 or 6/8 time, two simple styles may be suggested.

Pluck with the thumb, then pluck the three treble strings simultaneously to the rhythm dah-ti-dah-ti.

Or pluck with the thumb, then pluck the 3rd or 4th strings with the index finger; then pluck one or two strings with one or two fingers. Repeat, varying the combinations of strings, to the rhythm di-dle-i, di-dle-i (♪♪♩ , ♪♪♩).

(d) Another arpeggio pluck, suitable for dreamy quiet tunes, is made up of plucking with the thumb; then plucking the 3rd or 4th string with the index finger; then one or two treble strings with the 2nd and/or 3rd finger; then the 3rd or 4th string with the index finger again. Repeat *ad lib* to the rhythm dah-di-diddle, dah-di-diddle (♩♪♪ , ♩♪♪).

11 Plucking with the fingers

Scratching

For the first part of the measure you pluck a bass string with your thumb as before. For the second part of the stroke, you scratch down across the treble strings with the back of the index finger, then quickly scratch up again with the same finger across the same strings. Fine for fast mountain songs.

(a) In 2/4 songs, the rhythm will be dah-di-di (♩ ♪♪)

(b) In 3/4 songs, the rhythm will be
dah-di-di-di-di (♩ ♪♪ ♪♪)

(c) For a variation on this stroke which will introduce syncopation, after you have made the thumb pluck scratch up with the index finger, then down, then up again; then repeat the whole *ad lib* to the rhythm dah-dle-di-di (♩ ♪♪).

Picking

Picking the guitar (playing the melody against a background of chords) would be a subject for a treatise; here we can only describe two or three simple styles used among white and Negro folk musicians in the South.

(a) *The Church Lick.* In this method, as against the scratch described above, the thumb plays the melody of the song, instead of merely playing the bass notes in the chord. The style is made much more effective by the use of the following devices, favourites in the Southern States; they enhance the interest of any of the right-hand styles described in this section.

Hammering On: Strike one of the bass notes of your chord without first fretting it; then quickly fret it by bringing down the finger sharply on the string. For instance, in playing C, first pluck big A open, then hammer on with the third finger of the left hand on the third fret, then complete the scratch. The rhythm will be changed from dah-di-di (♩ ♪♪) to
dah-dle-di-di (♪♪ ♪♪). Any string within the chord can be hammered on in this fashion, and the device, used with subtlety, can give a hot, hillbilly lick to various types of accompaniment.

Pulling Off: This is the reverse of hammering on. After a string is plucked, the finger of the left hand that is fretting the string is pulled off with sufficient force to make the string sound the open note. For example, if you are playing E minor and pluck the fourth string, you first get E, then by pulling off you get D. The rhythmic effect is the same as above.

Bass Runs: There is an endless number of bass runs which can be played. Here we can only give a few examples from the key of C, to start you off. In a simple 2/4 accompaniment, for instance, instead of beginning with the C chord, play G–A–C, then the C chord; then in ascending run play D–E–F, then the F chord; then F–D–C, then C chord; then C–B–G, then the G chord; and so on.

(b) *Clawhammer Style.* In this style, the thumb picks out a conventional bass, while the index finger picks out the melody of the song.

As the thumb plucks down on a bass string, the index finger simultaneously plucks up on the first note of the melody; then the thumb strums down across all the strings; the thumb plucks a bass string, as the index finger picks out the second note of the melody; the thumb strums down again. This is repeated *ad lib* to the rhythm dah-di, dah-di (♩ ♩ , ♩ ♩). If the melody requires, the finger may pluck up on the 2nd and 4th steps as well; in this case, the thumb stroke is shorter.

It may be that the main accents of the tune may fall on the off-beats, so that the index finger may be picking out the tune in between the thumb strokes. This requires a certain degree of skill which will certainly come if the player has practised playing melodies with his fingers, while training his right thumb to play a smooth rhythm.

(c) *Double Thumb Picking.* Here again the melody is picked out by the index finger against a steady bass beat, but in this case the bass consists of a series of single notes.

With an E chord, set the thumb plucking alternately the bass E and the E on the fretted 4th string. Practise this until the thumb swings freely between these two notes in a steady dah-di, dah-di rhythm (♩ ♩ , ♩ ♩). Then pick out the tune with the index finger on the treble strings, while the steady beat continues on the bass strings; the result is a continuous flow of broken chords with the tune singing above them. If the melody is an off-beat one, the melodic accents will often fall in between the regular thumb plucks in patterns like
daddle-di-di, daddle-di-di (♪♪♩ , ♪♪♩).

The really skilful player, after a great deal of practice will bring the middle finger into play. Then, if he is using bass runs and hammering on, he will be playing in the best mountain style. (An essential aid in all this is the study of the recordings recommended in Appendix 2.)

Special Licks for Negro Spirituals, Blues, and Worksongs

The Negroes have been the principal creators of American guitar style. What have so far been described are Southern white licks – which are imitations of Negro folk guitar, and which can serve to accompany Negro songs quite well.

True Negro folk guitar is much too complex to be described in a brief guide, and yet the learner can set out upon the right road if he learns the following three licks, all of which are used by Negro folk musicians, though in a subtler manner than can be expressed in words or notes. (Here again, I recommend the study of recordings.)

Often Negro musicians damp the strings at a certain point in each measure and shift the accent to this damped- or off-beat to give their songs a syncopated or rocking feeling. They damp the strings immediately after they are plucked or scratched or strummed, using the palm or the heel of the hand. Another way of damping is to raise the fingers of the left hand which are fretting the chord, thus deadening the strings. (In the following descriptions the syllable 'yup' indicates the damped beat.)

(a) *The Damped Strum.* This is useful for almost any 2/4 Negro song.

Strum down across several bass strings; strum down across treble strings with thumb or fingers; damp the treble strings immediately. Repeat these three steps *ad lib* to the rhythm dah-dyup, dah-dyup (♩ ♩ , ♩ ♩).

150

(b) *The Damped Scratch*. At fast tempo this is good for songs like *John Henry*; at slow tempo it is good for rhythmic spirituals.

Thumb strokes down; finger scratches up lightly; then finger scratches down hard – damp immediately; then finger scratches up. Repeat these four steps *ad lib* to the rhythm daddle-dyup-di, daddle-dyup-di (♫ ♫, ♫ ♫).

(c) *An easy blues lick*. There are scores of ways to play the blues, but this is about the easiest lick which suits blues and worksongs.

Strum down across four or five strings with the thumb – damp at once; strum back up with the index finger across two or three treble strings. Repeat these two steps *ad lib* to the rhythm dyup-di, dyup-di (♩♪, ♩♪).

Most blues players keep some steady rhythm like this going behind their songs, but play very quietly and well damped down. Then, in the spaces between phrases or at the end of lines, they introduce a great variety of runs, slurred notes, melodic comments, etc. A few of the simplest and easiest of these effects are the following.

The thumb stroke is taken over by the index finger, which strokes upward across the treble strings in a series of four measures of dup-di-dup-di-dup-di-dup-di (♫ ♫ ♫ ♫).

Or, in a series of triplets, dup-diddy, dup-diddy, dup-diddy, dup-diddy (♪♫, ♪♫, ♪♫, ♪♫).

The melody of the blues can be picked out in part, with the blue notes slurred. There are two principal ways of slurring notes: the finger that frets the note pushes or pulls the string to one side when it has been struck, making the string cry out a blue note; or the fretting finger runs up or down one string after it has been struck, so that the note is slurred by a full tone, or some other suitable interval.

Appendix 2

SELECTED LIST OF RECORDINGS OF AMERICAN FOLK MUSIC

DISCOGRAPHY

This is a brief and selective list of American folk-song recordings issued in Britain and the U.S.A. Unless otherwise stated, the records are or were issued in both countries by the company shown; *remarks in italics apply to the U.S.A. only*.

BROONZY, Big Bill (Mississippi blues singer with excellent urban style)
'Big Bill Broonzy Sings Country Blues' (Folkways 2326)
'Songs and Story' (Folkways 3586)
'The Blues' (Mercury ZEP 10093, *Mercury 36137*)
'An evening with Big Bill' (Tempo Yep TA P23, *not released in U.S.*)
'Big Bill Blues' (Vogue LAE 12009, *not released in U.S.*)
Melodisc Epm 765 (*not released in U.S.*)
'Last Session' (HMV CLP 1544, 1551, 1562; *Verve 3001–3* (three LPs)

BLIND BLAKE (Blake was considered the finest of all blues guitarists in his time)
Collector JFL 2001
Collector JEL 4 (with Rambling Thomas); *no U.S. issues available*

CARAWAN, Guy (a good young singer of folk songs; fine banjo and guitar)
'Songs' (three LPs, Folkways 3544, 3548, 3552)
Not released in U.S.:
'Mountain Songs and Banjo Tunes' (Topic 10-T24)
'Guy Carawan Sings' (Collector EP JEA 4)

DRIFTWOOD, Jimmie (a true folk bard from the Ozarks, but subject to modern influences; some wonderful songs; plays the mouthbow)
'The Wilderness Road' (RCA LP RD 27144, *Victor LPM 1994, stereo LSP 1994*)

ELLIOTT, Jack (a fine folk-style guitar player; has learnt Woody Guthrie's singing style)
No records at present available;
'Woody Guthrie Blues' (Topic T5)
'Jack Takes the Floor' (Topic 10-T15)
'The Rambling Boys' (Topic 10-T14)

FULLER, Jesse (a Southern Negro folk-singer who lives in San Francisco)
Good Time Jazz LA G 12159, *Good Time Jazz 12031*
'The Rambling Boys' (Topic 10-T14)

GOLDEN GATE QUARTET (a superb and sophisticated folk quartet from Virginia)
Columbia EP SEG 7700 (*not released in U.S.*)

GUTHRIE, Woody, and Cisco HOUSTON (the best modern folk-singers of the Southwest)
'Bound for Glory' (Folkways 2481)
'Dust Bowl Ballads' (Folkways 2011)
'Bound for Glory' (Topic 12-T31, *not released in U.S.*)
Melodisc MLP 516 (with Sonny Terry)
Melodisc EPM 7-91
Melodisc MLP 12-106
The various Melodisc releases are all to be found on two U.S. LPs: Stinson 44 and 53.

HOPKINS, Lightning (a fine urban folk guitarist and singer from Texas)
'Lightning Hopkins' (Folkways 3822)
'The Rooster Crowed in England' (Dobell's '77' LA 12-1, *not released in U.S.*)
'Lightning Hopkins in New York' (*Candid 8010*)
'Lightnin' and Blues' (*Herald 1012*)

IVES, Burl (an accomplished and polished folk guitarist and singer with Midwestern roots)
'Men' (Ace of Hearts AH53, *Decca 8125*)
There are many LPs by Burl Ives in the British and American catalogues

JEFFERSON, Blind Lemon (the first and finest of all professional folk blues singers)
'Folk Blues' vol. 1 (*River-side 125*) } *available only U.S. at present*
'Folk Blues' vol. 2 (*River-side 136*) }
Collector JEL 8 (with Buddy Boy Hawkins)

LEDBETTER, Huddie (LEADBELLY) (the greatest blues singer from the Southwest)
'Last Sessions' (Folkways FA 2941 and FA 2942)
'Leadbelly's Legacy' (Folkways 2004, 2014, 2024, 2034)
'The Rock Island Line' (RCA-RCX 146, *not released in U.S.*)
'Good Morning Blues' (RCA RD 7567)
Melodisc EPM 7-82; 7-77
Melodisc MLP 511; MLP 512; MLP 515
The various Melodisc releases are all drawn from four Stinson LPs: Stinson 17, 19, 48, 51

LOMAX, Alan
'Murderer's Home' (*Tradition 1020*)
'Songs from Texas' (Melodisc EPM 7-88,)
'Texas Folksongs' (*Tradition 1029*)
Readers are also referred to the seven-volume set of field recordings, *Southern Folk Heritage*, released in Britain by London and in the U.S. by Atlantic

McCOLL, Ewan, and A. L. LLOYD (finest male singers of folk songs in Britain)
Shanties and Sea Songs (Topic T 7 and T 8, *not available in U.S.*)
'Blow Boys Blow' (*Tradition 1026*)

MONROE, Bill, and THE BLUE GRASS BOYS (one of the best bluegrass groups)
'Bluegrass Ramble' (Brunswick LAT 8511, stereo STA 8511; *Decca 4266, stereo 74266*)

RAMBLING THOMAS (a real Mississippi-country blues singer, recorded in the early thirties)
Collector JEL 4 (with Blind Blake, *not available in U.S.*)

RITCHIE, Jean (the superb Kentucky mountain singer, with dulcimer)
'Ritchie Family of Kentucky' (Folkways 2316)
'Jean Ritchie' (*Elektra 125*)
'Best of Jean Ritchie' (*Prestige-International 13003*)

RODGERS, Jimmie (one of the earliest and most interesting of the hillbilly singers)
'Never No Mo'' (RCA RD 27138, *Victor LPM 1232*)
'Train Whistle Blues' (RCA RD 27110, *Victor LPM 1650*
'My Rough and Rowdy Ways' (RCA RD 27203, *Victor LPM 2112*)

SEEGER, Peggy (one of America's most talented singers and performers of folk-songs)
Folkways 2005 (with her sisters and brother)
Topic 10-T9
'Come Along John' (Topic TOP 18, with sisters)
'Shine Like a Star' (Topic TOP 38, with sisters)
Some of the Topic material can be found on the Folkways issue.

SEEGER, Pete (the Favourite American singer of folk songs; wonderful banjo player; his tutors are essential)
'Banjo Tutor' (Folkways 8203)
'The Guitar Guide' (Topic 12-T20)
'Pete and Five Strings' (Topic TOP 33)

TAMPA RED and GEORGIA TOM (a fascinating professional folk duo from Memphis)
Collector JEL 3 (*not U.S.*)

TERRY, Sonny, and Brownie McGHEE (Sonny, the best harmonica player; Brownie, a fine blues musician; good modern folk blues)
'Harmonica Blues' (Topic 10-T30, also on Folkways 2035)
Topic 12-T29 (also on Folkways 2327)

WATERS, Muddy (great Mississippi blues singer)
'The Best of Muddy Waters' (*Chess 1427*)
'Mississippi Blues' (Vogue EPV 1046, *not available U.S.*)

WHITE, Josh (fine Negro singer; superb guitarist; sophisticated style)
'The Josh White Stories' (*ABC-Paramount LP 124 and 166*)
There are many LPs by Josh White in the British and American catalogues.

YANCEY, Jimmy (the father of boogie-woogie piano)
'Pure Blues' (with Mama Yancey) (*Atlantic 1283*)

155

INDEX OF TITLES

INDEX OF FIRST LINES

158

Other Penguin Books on Music

THE PENGUIN BOOK OF CHRISTMAS CAROLS

Edited by Elizabeth Poston

Fifty Christmas carols – music arranged by Elizabeth Poston, with a simple vocal or instrumental descant for each one. Carols included range from 'Hark! the herald angels' to folklore carols culled from English, French, and Russian sources. *Also available:* The Second Penguin Book of Christmas Carols

THE PENGUIN BOOK OF LIEDER

S. S. Prawer

The texts – with line by line English translations – of many of the best-known Lieder from Haydn to Hindemith. An introduction covering the relation of music to poetry in German song, biographical notes on the poets and composers, and a discography are also included. *A Penguin Reference Book*

THE PENGUIN AUSTRALIAN SONG BOOK

Compiled by J. S. Manifold

Eighty songs divided into the following sections: Seamen and Transports; Immigrants and Diggers; The Bushrangers; Pastoral Australia; The Nomads; The Poets.

CHAMBER MUSIC

Edited by Alec Robertson

Deals with musical works ranging from duets to octets composed between the beginning of the 18th century and the present day are discussed. Numerous musical examples are included. *A Pelican Book*

CHORAL MUSIC

Edited by Arthur Jacobs

Twenty American and British experts contribute to this volume which traces the history of music for human voices from the year A.D. 1,000 to the present day. *A Pelican Book*

THE CONCERTO

Edited by Ralph Hill

The development of the concerto form from Bach to William Walton. Well-known piano, violin, and cello concertos of the current repertoire are analysed and illustrated with a wealth of musical examples. *A Pelican Book*

THE SYMPHONY

Edited by Robert Simpson

Volume 1: Haydn to Dvořák
Volume 2: Elgar to the Present Day

A comprehensive introduction to the whole symphonic scene. A team of distinguished contributors provides a connected, unified study of all major composers who have 'attempted to achieve in orchestral work the highest state of organization of which music is capable'. In two excellent introductions Robert Simpson analyses the essence of symphonic form. *Pelican Books*

MUSICAL INSTRUMENTS THROUGH THE AGES

Edited by Anthony Baines

Describes the origins of the various musical instruments as well as the music written for them. Illustrated. *A Pelican Book*

A NEW DICTIONARY OF MUSIC

Arthur Jacobs

A basic, up-to-date reference book covering orchestral, solo, choral, and chamber music, as well as the opera and the musical aspects of the ballet. Includes entries on composers, musical works, orchestras, performers, conductors, instruments, and technical terms. *A Penguin Reference Book*

THE PELICAN HISTORY OF MUSIC

Edited by Alec Robertson and Denis Stevens

1. ANCIENT FORMS TO POLYPHONY.   Deals with music from the earliest known forms through the first half of the 15th century and compares Western music with that which developed in other parts of the world. *A Pelican Book*

2. RENAISSANCE AND BAROQUE.   Continues the story of Western music from the mid-15th century to 1760, with special emphasis on the social and artistic environment of Europe during the period. Both volumes are illustrated and contain many musical examples. *A Pelican Book*

3. CLASSICAL AND ROMANTIC.   This volume is mainly concerned with the eighteenth and nineteenth centuries, but works by Mahler, Bloch, Bax and others are discussed in a coda. *A Pelican Book*